I0488712

Experts Share Secrets: How To Draw Eyes Volume 1

Expert Advice on Drawing Eyes Correctly

How to Draw Eyes

By : Gala Publication

Published By :

Gala Publication

© Copyright 2015 – Gala Publication

ISBN-13: **978-1522785309**
ISBN-10: **1522785302**

Table of Contents

COMIC BOOK
EYES

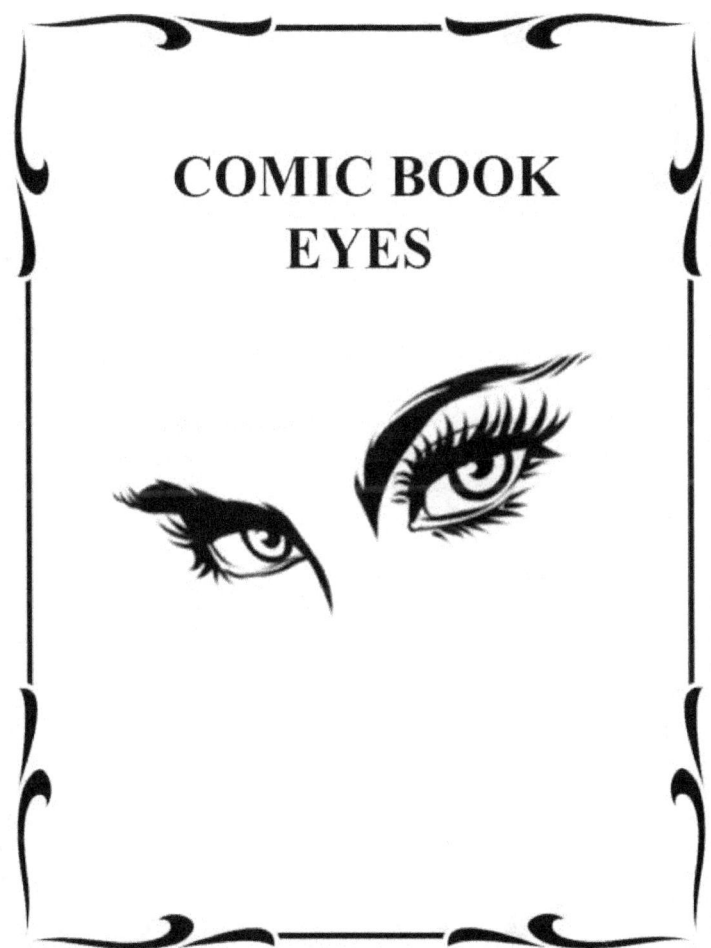

STEP 1

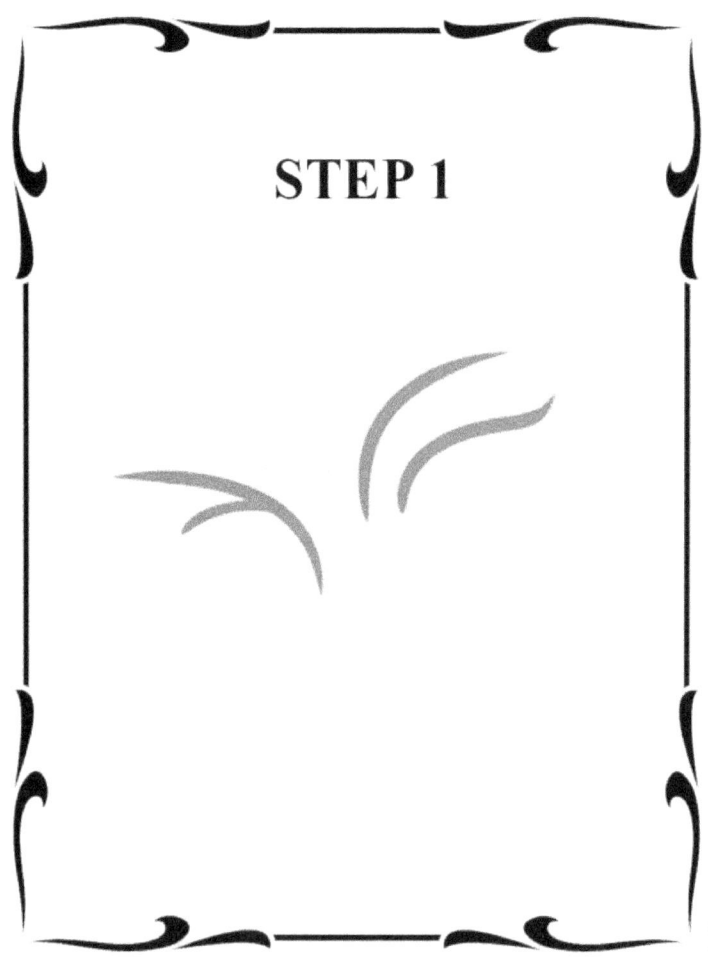

STEP 2

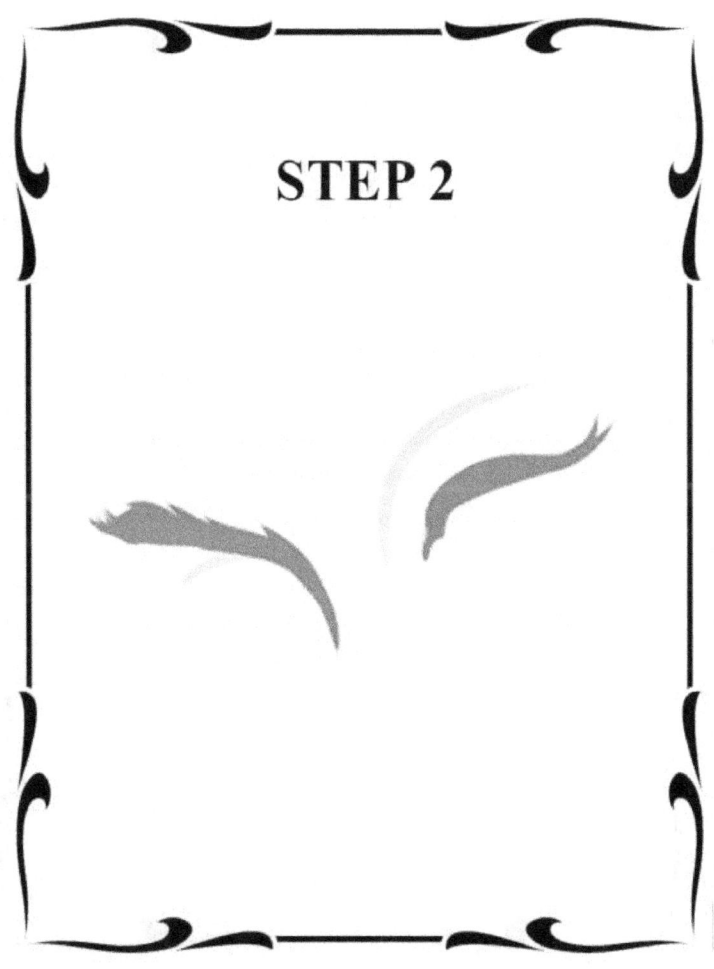

STEP 3

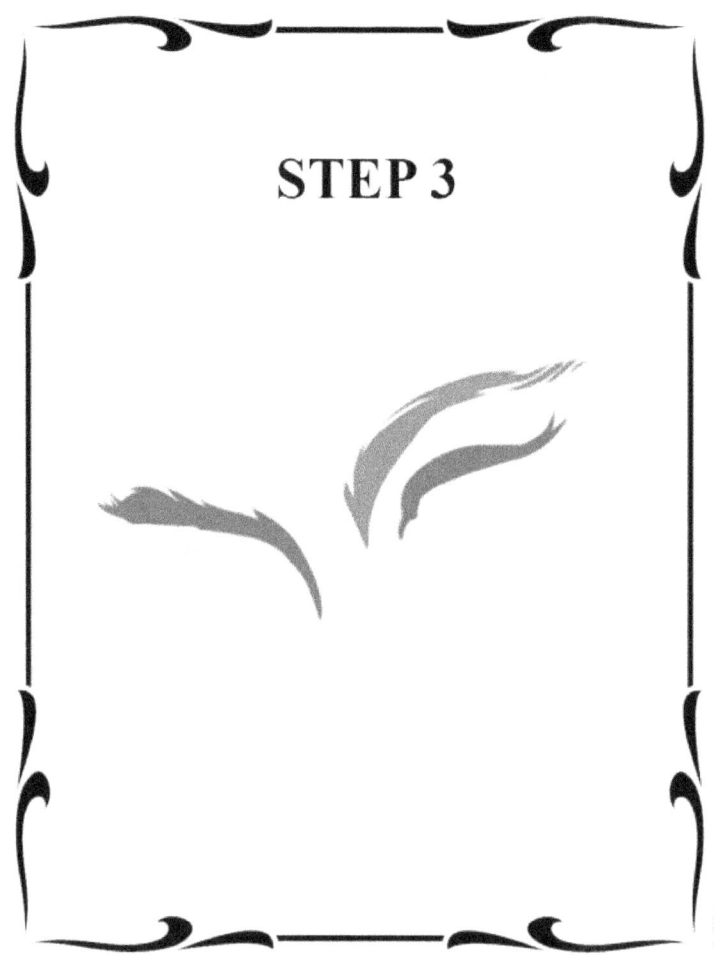

STEP 4

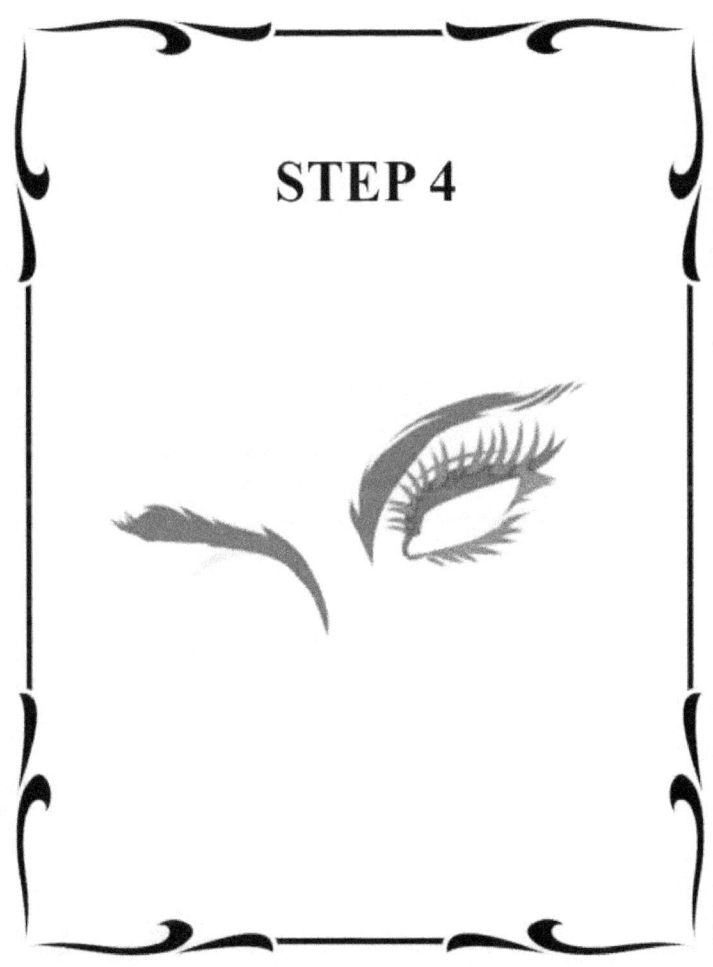

STEP 5

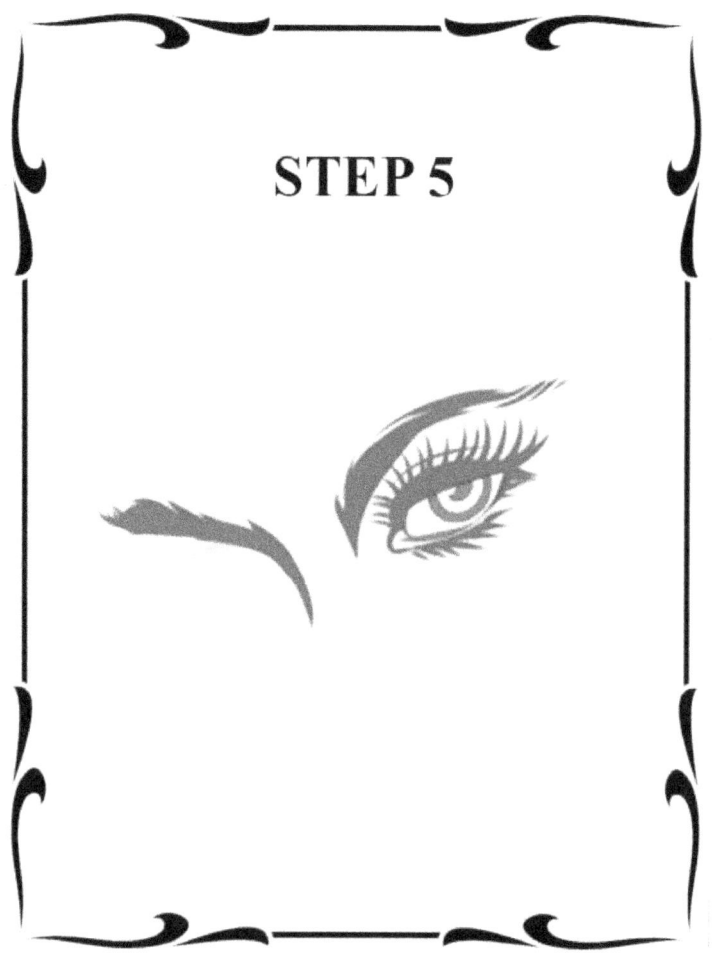

STEP 6

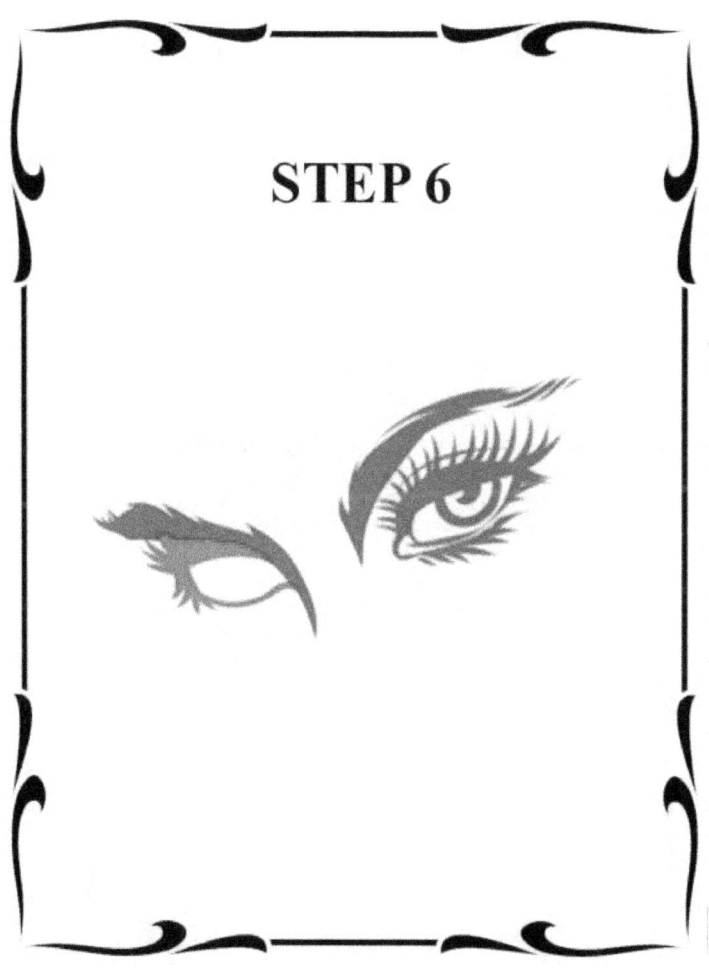

STEP 7

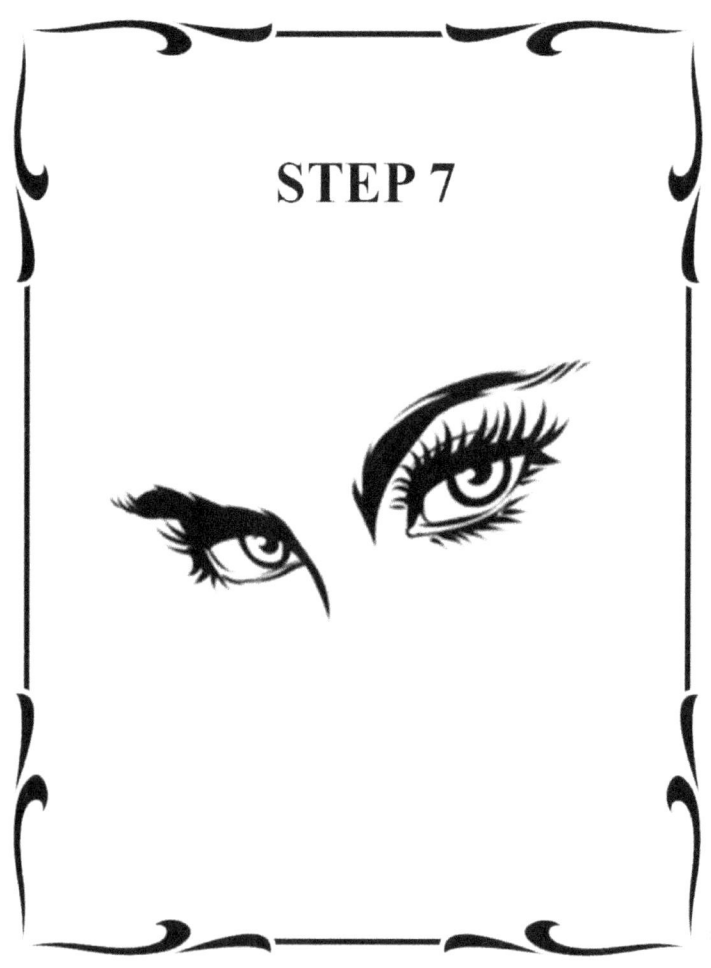

DARK EYES

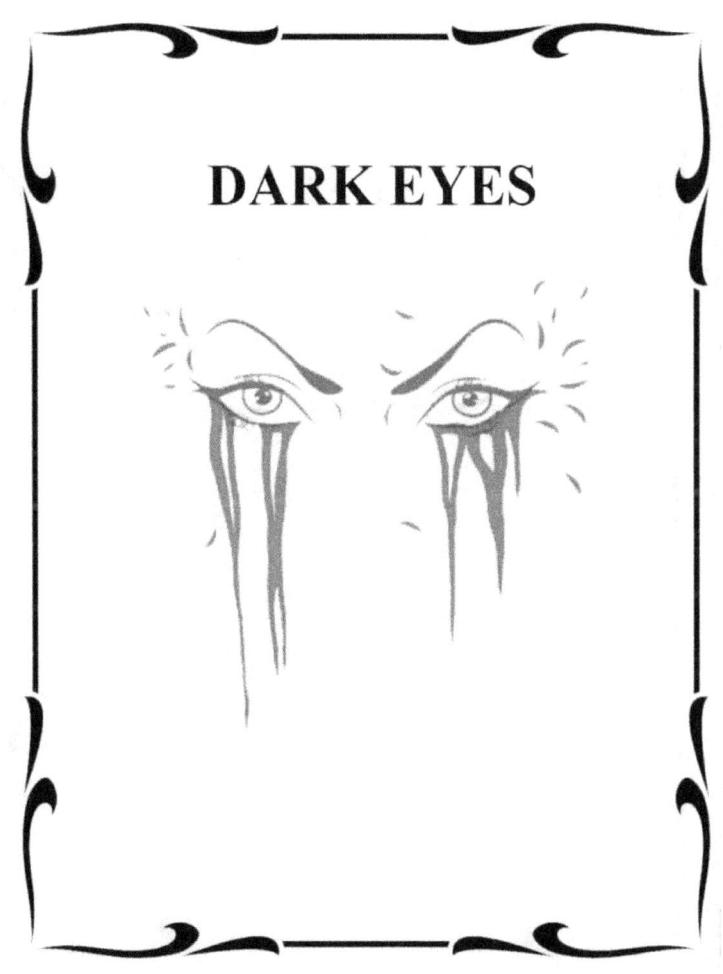

STEP 1

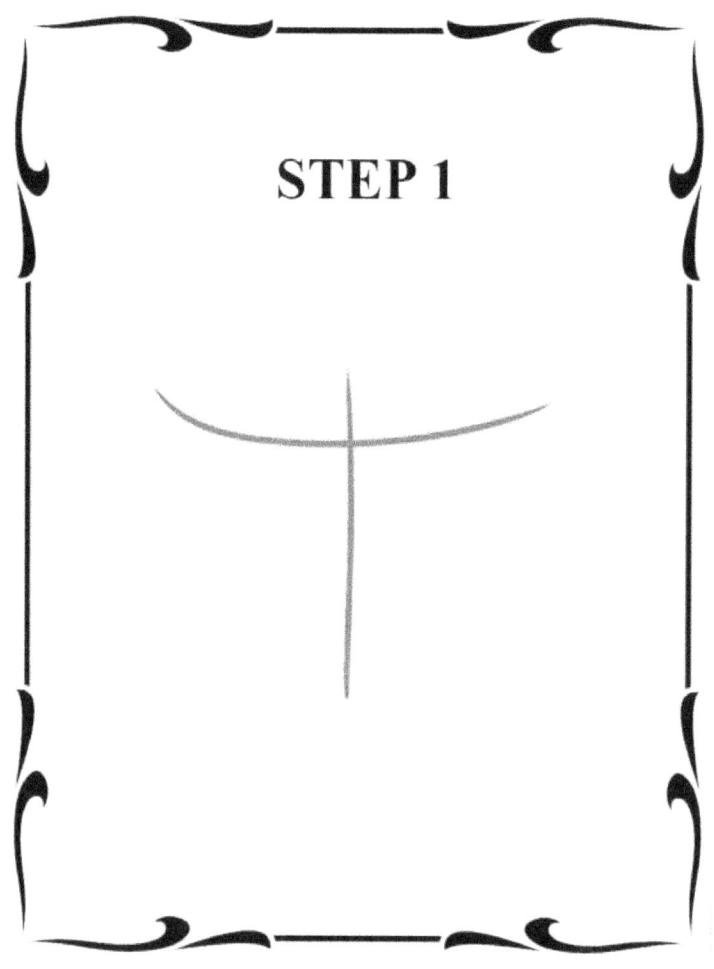

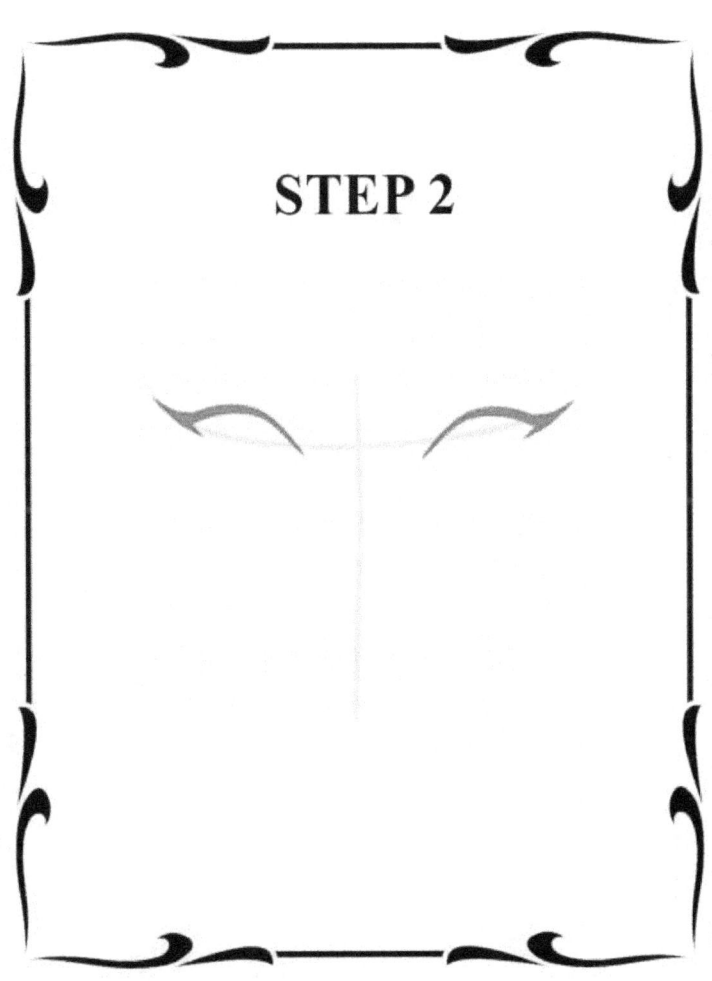

STEP 2

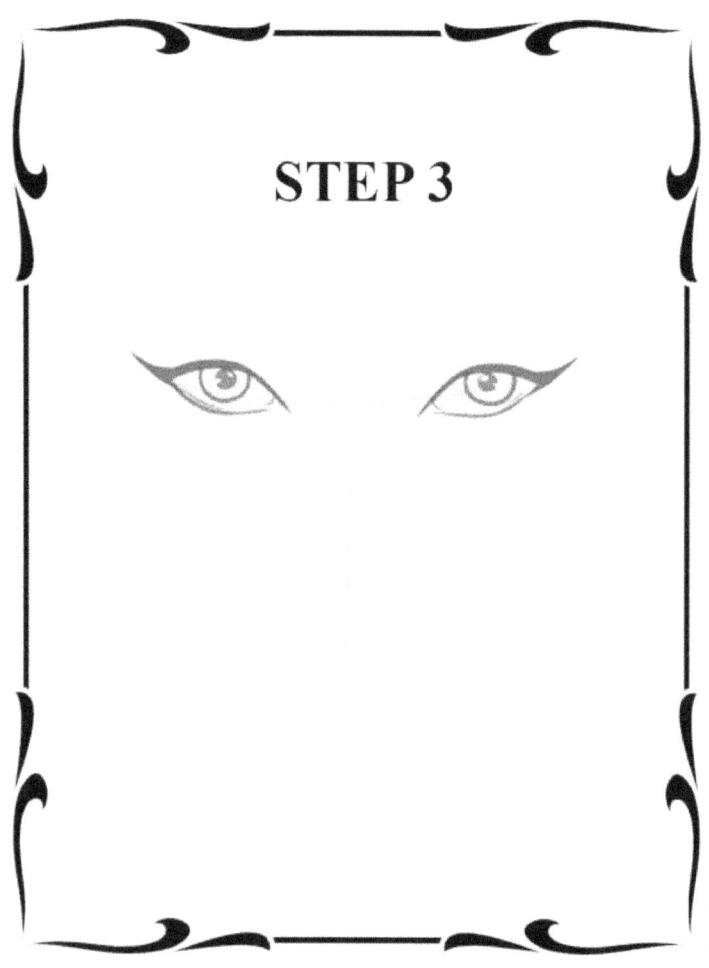

STEP 3

STEP 4

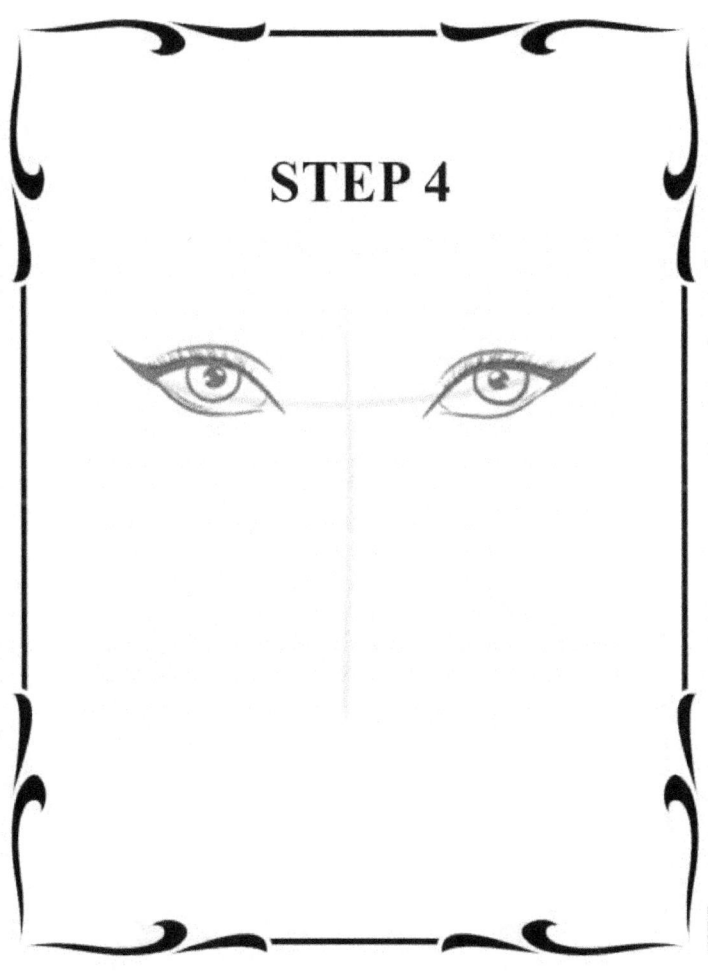

STEP 5

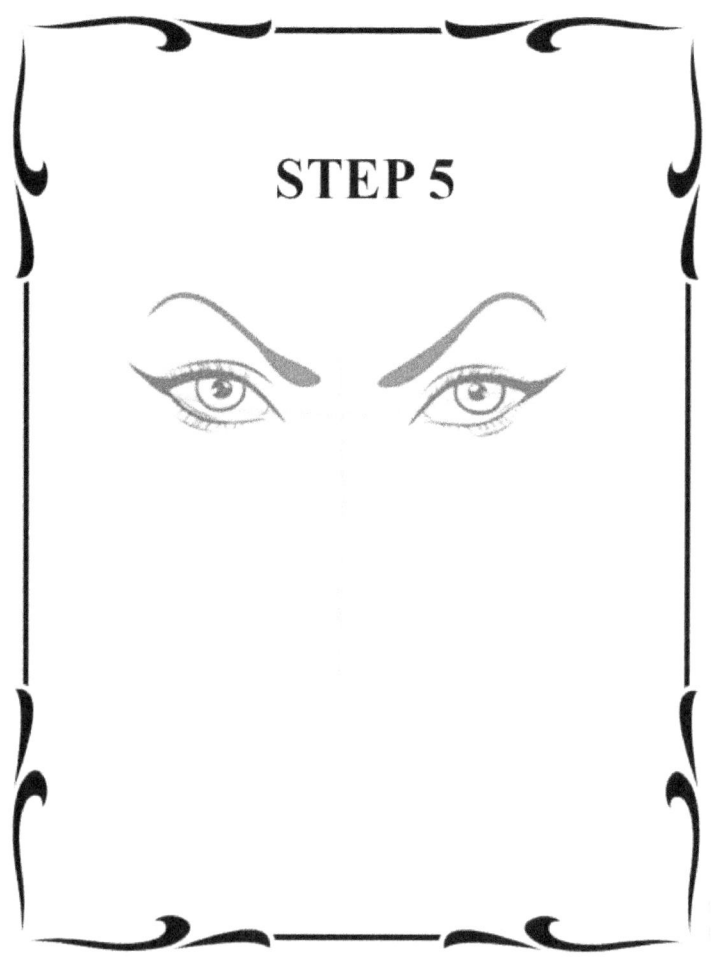

STEP 6

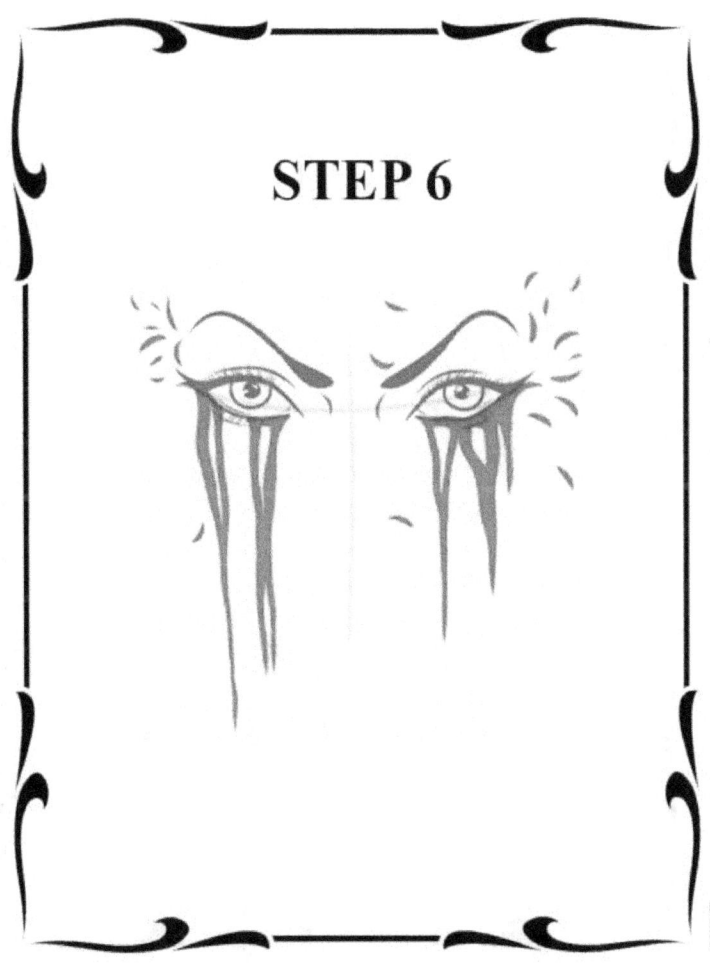

STEP 7

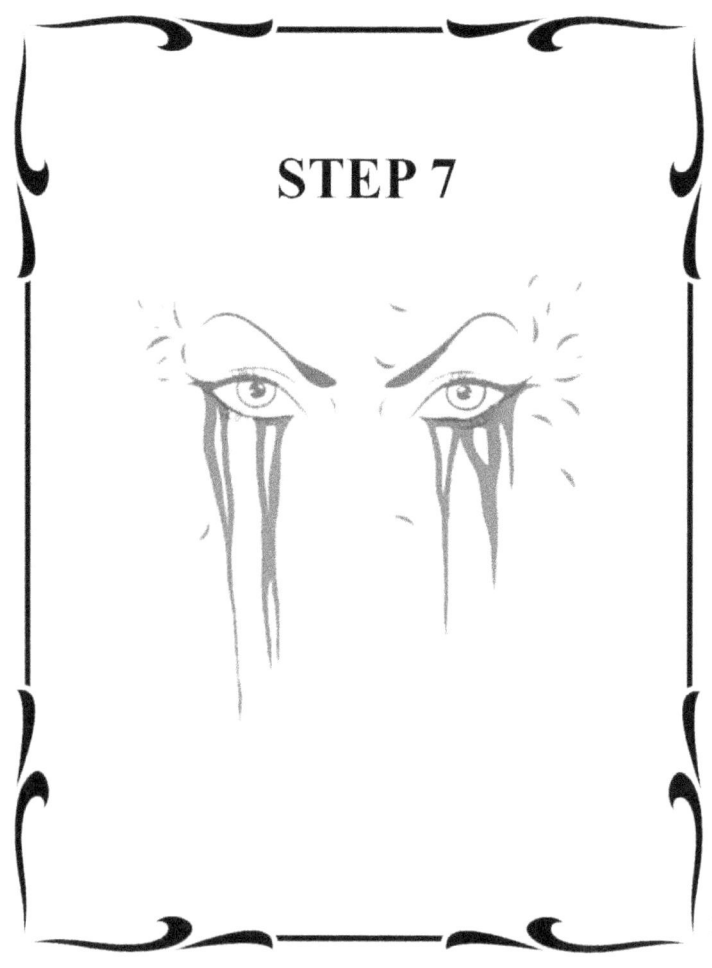

FANTASY EYES

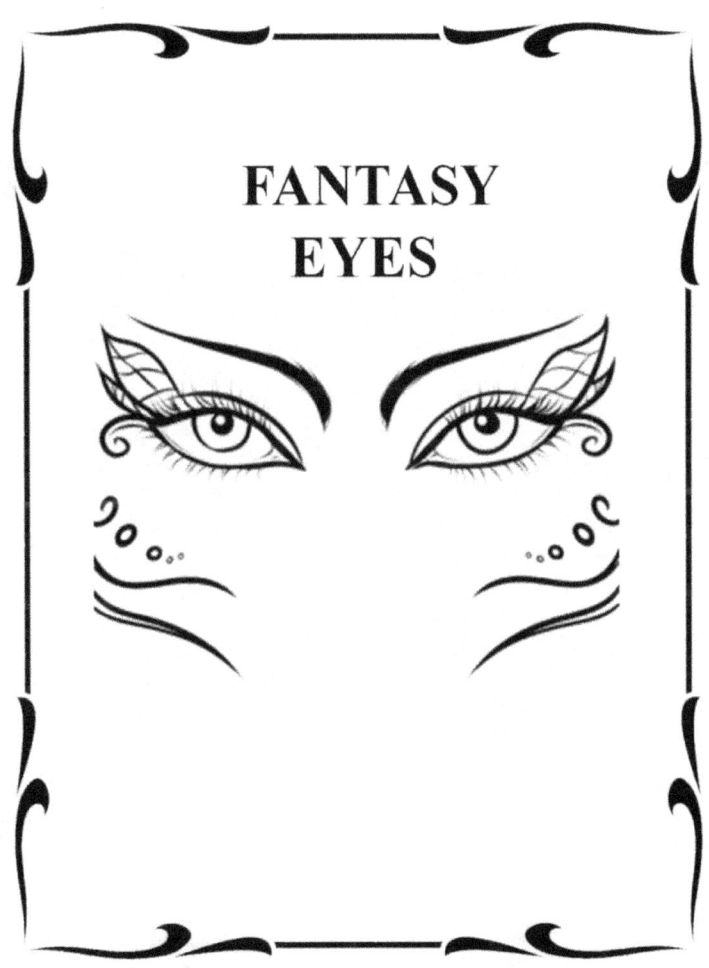

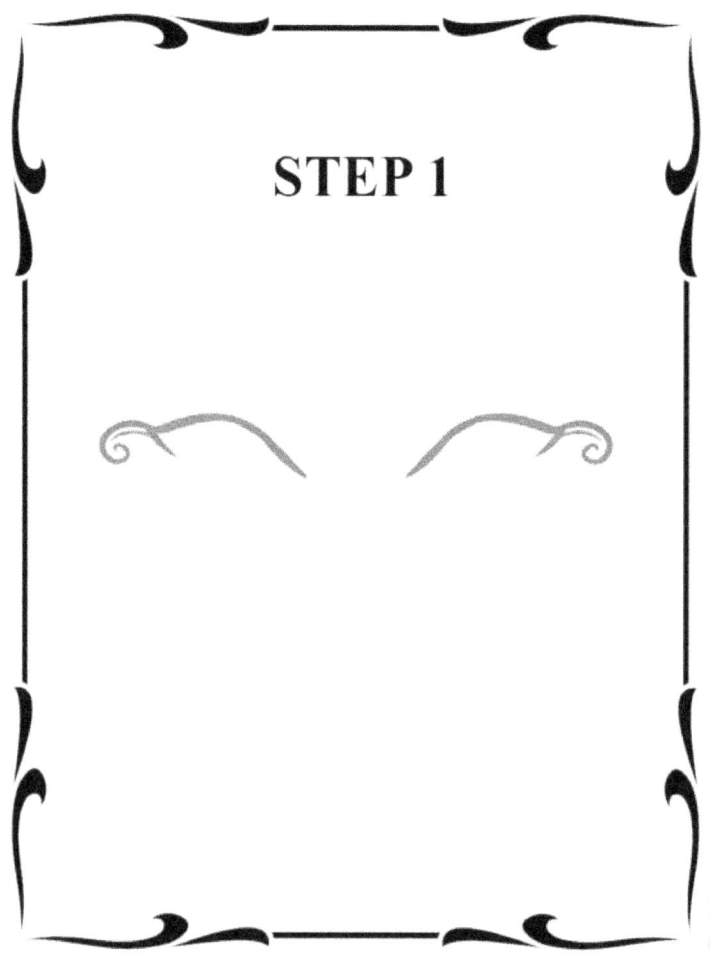

STEP 1

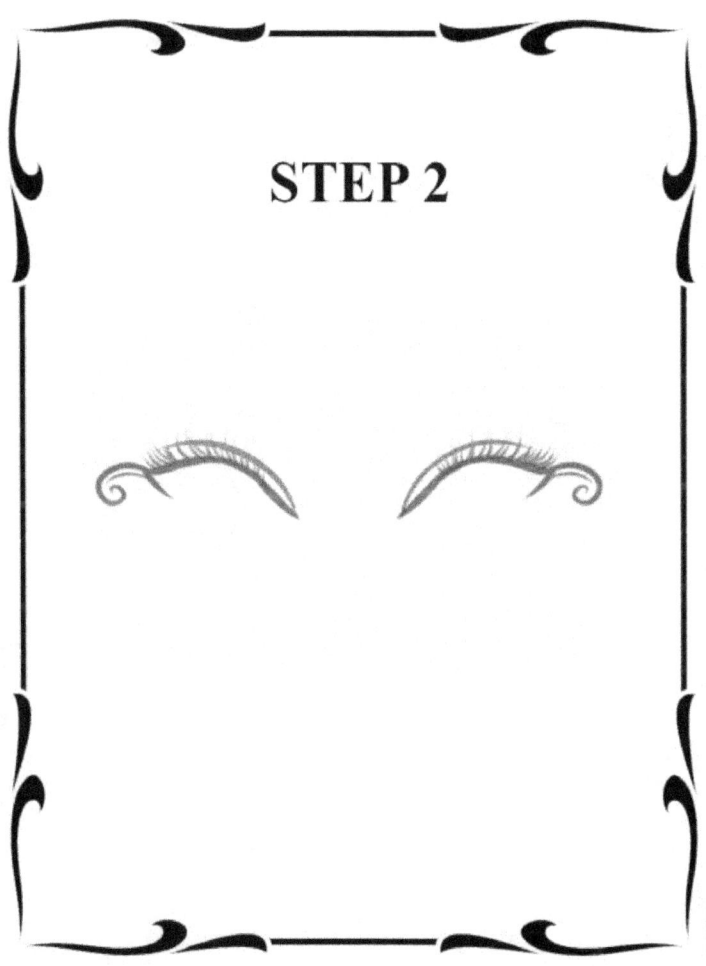

STEP 2

STEP 3

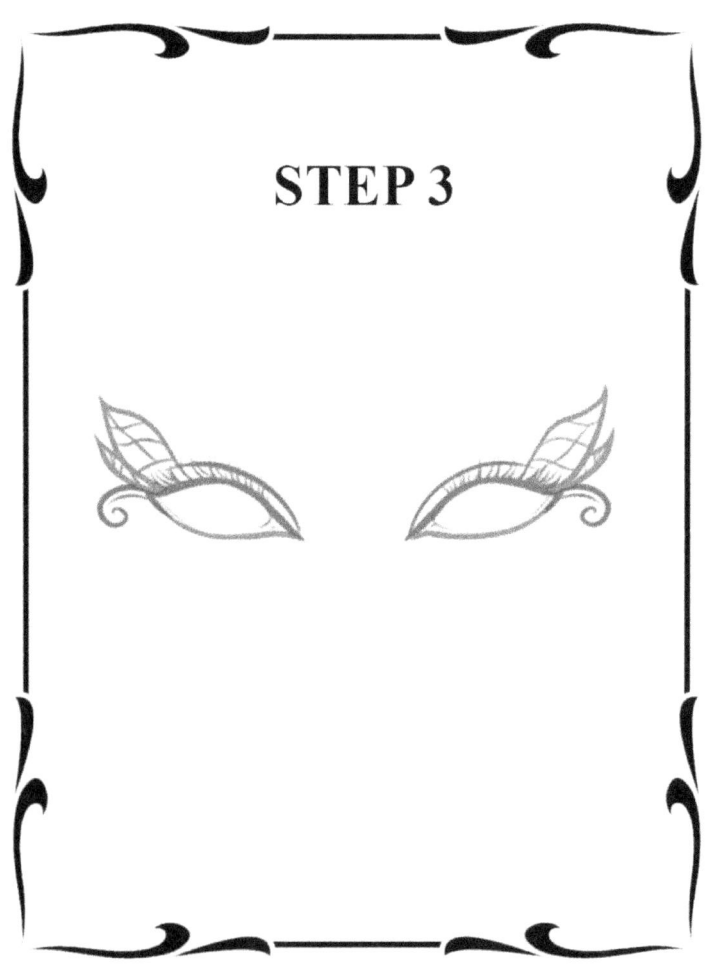

STEP 4

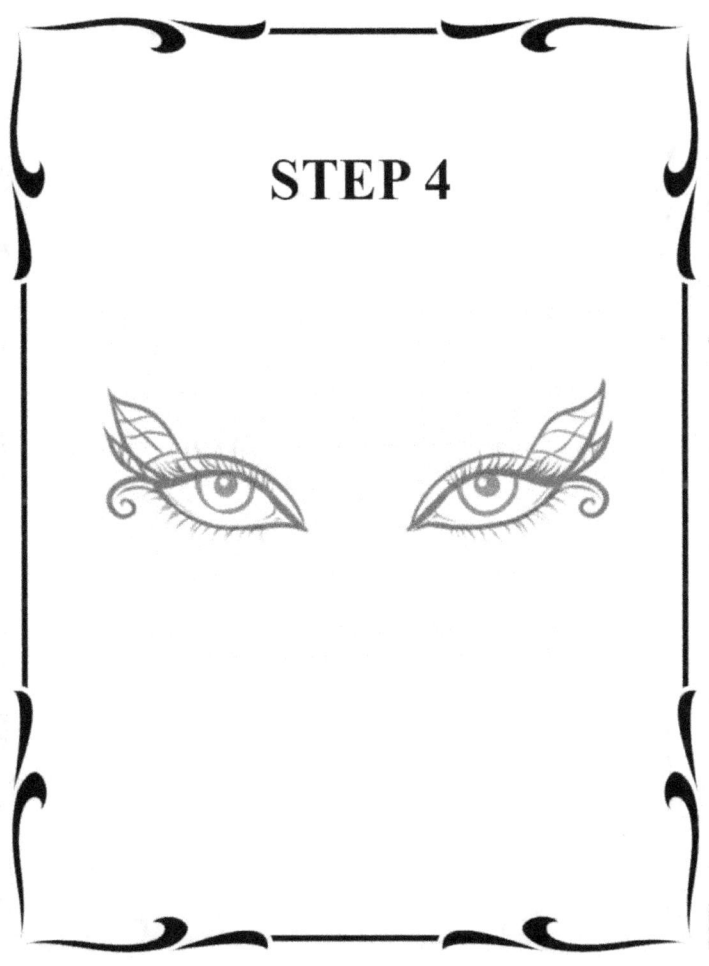

STEP 5

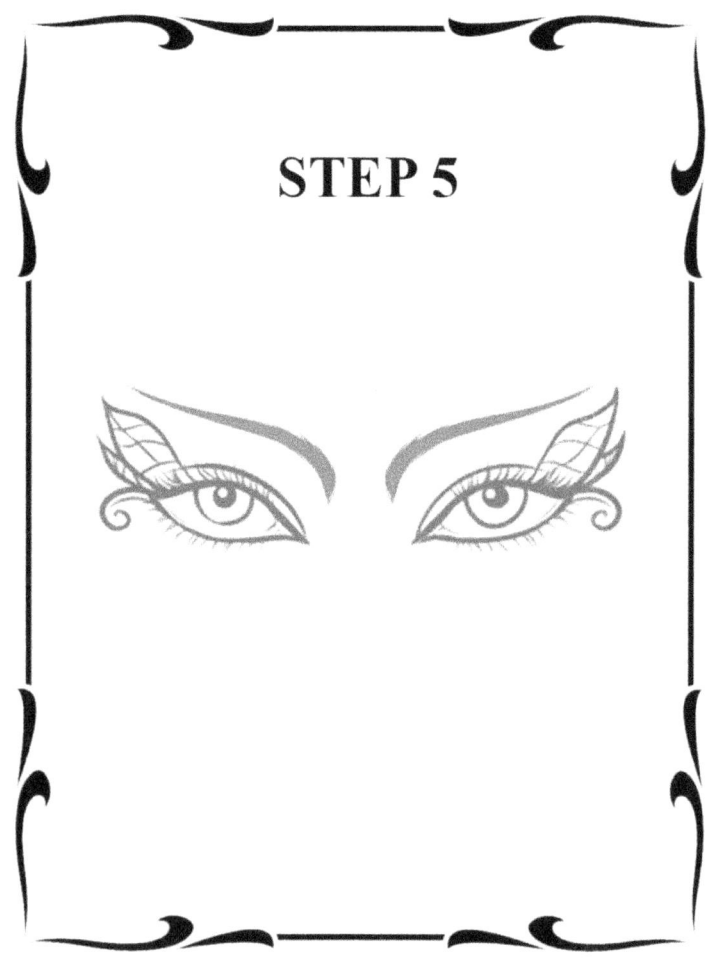

STEP 6

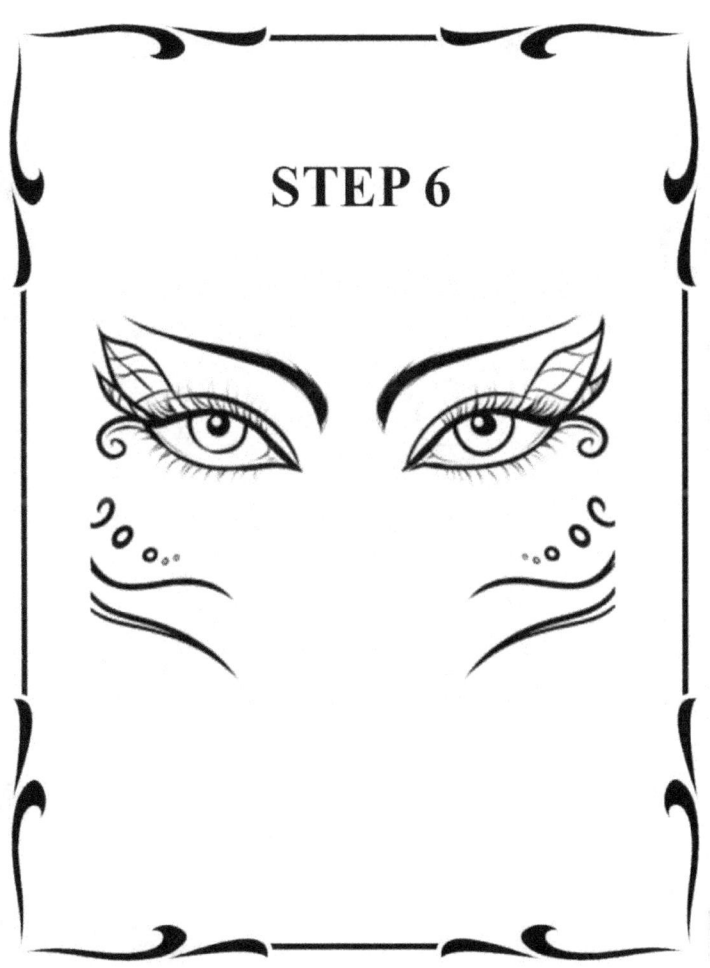

RED EYES

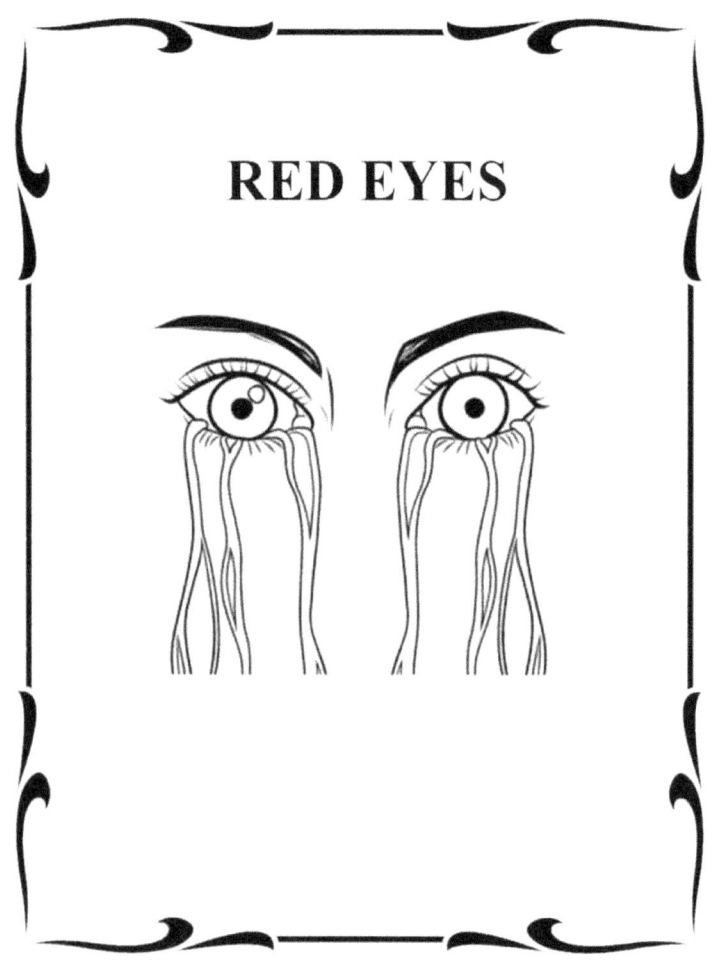

STEP 1

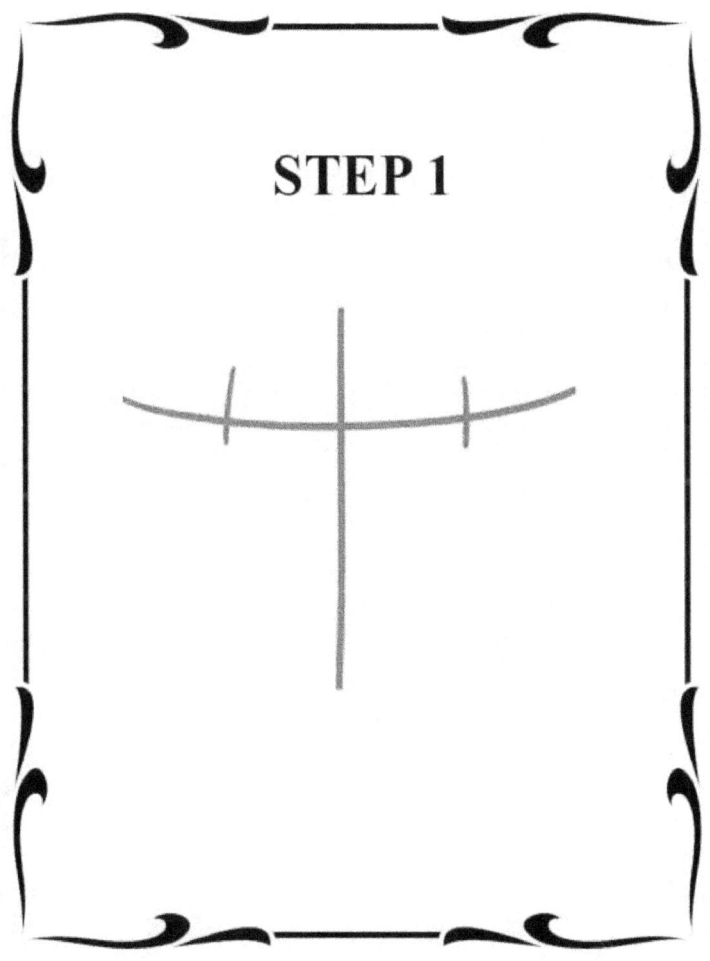

STEP 2

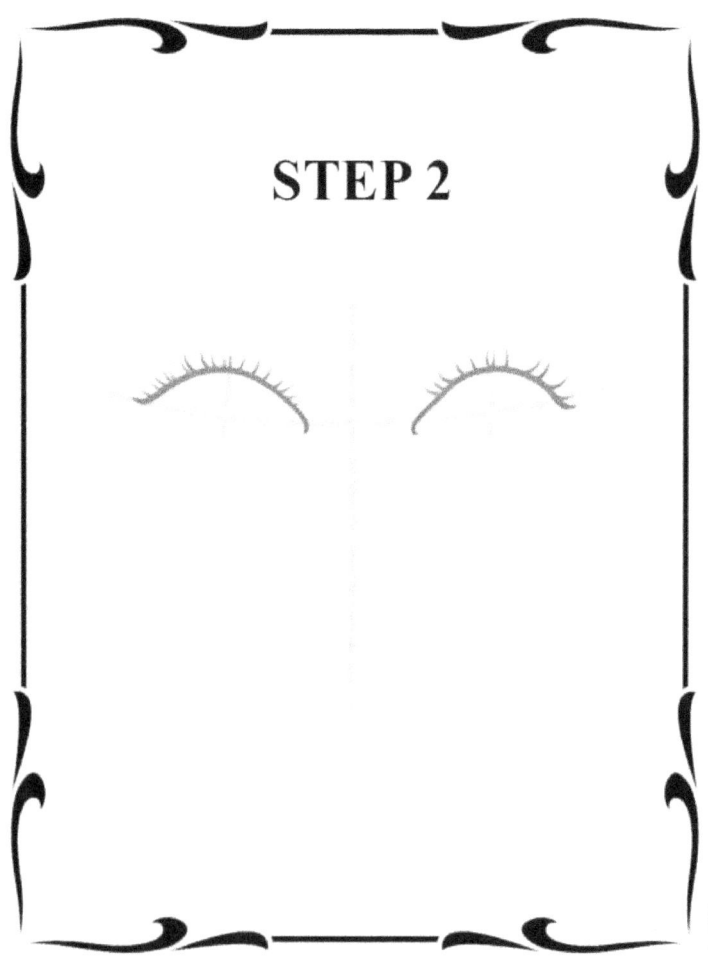

STEP 3

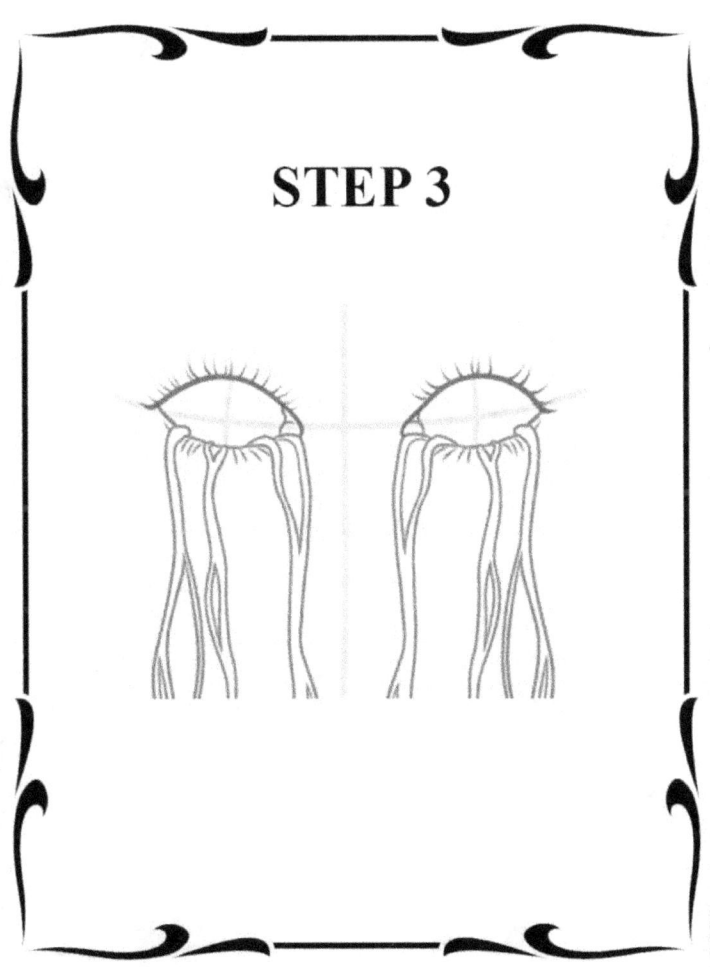

STEP 4

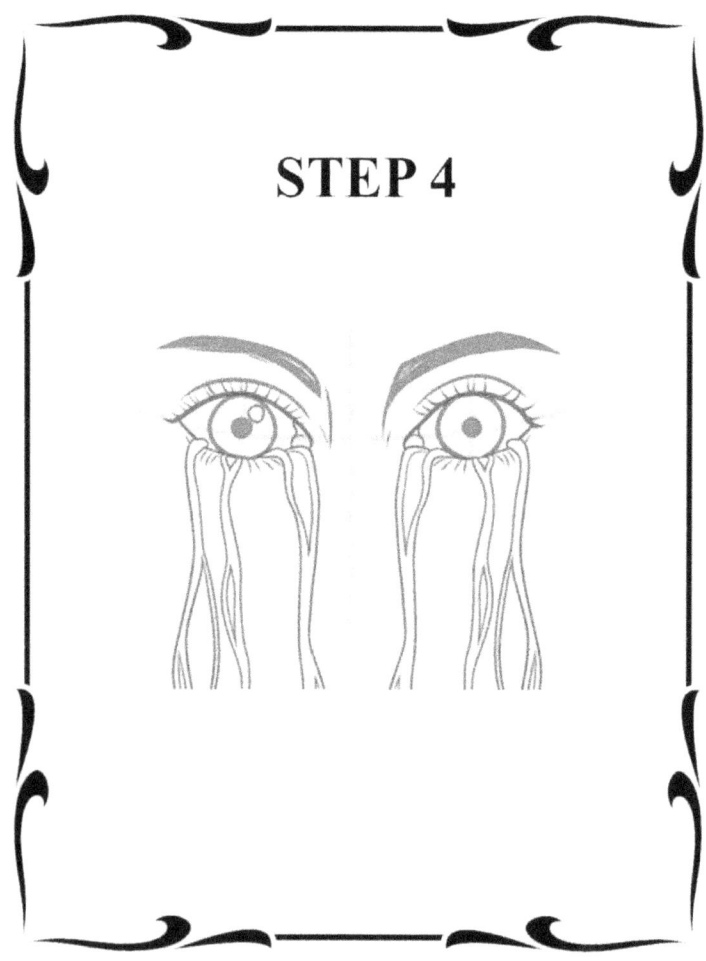

STEP 5

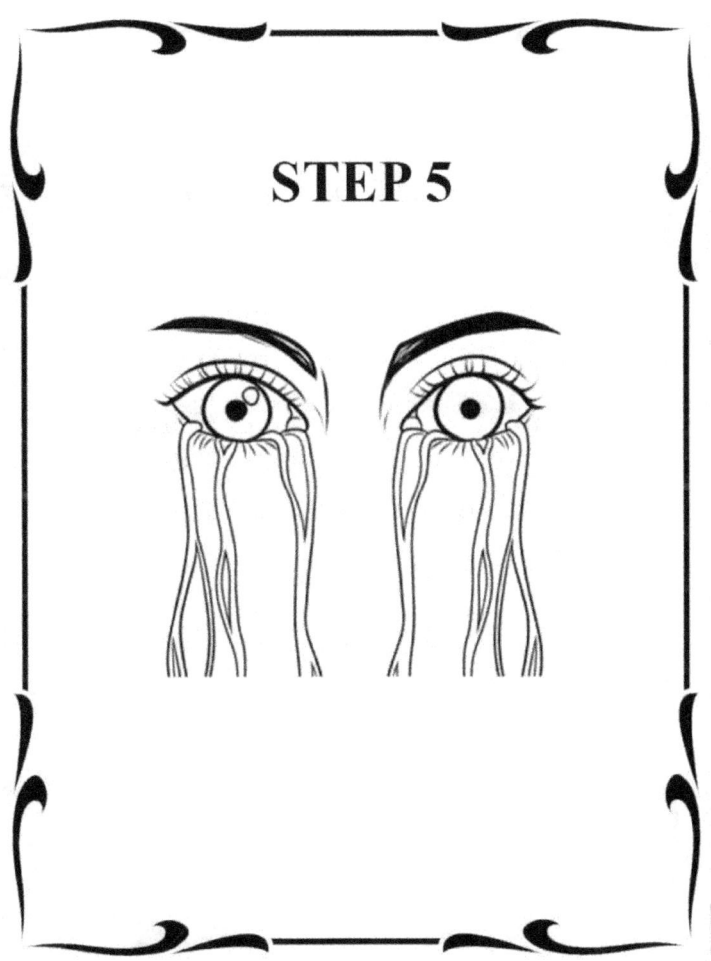

SCARED EYES

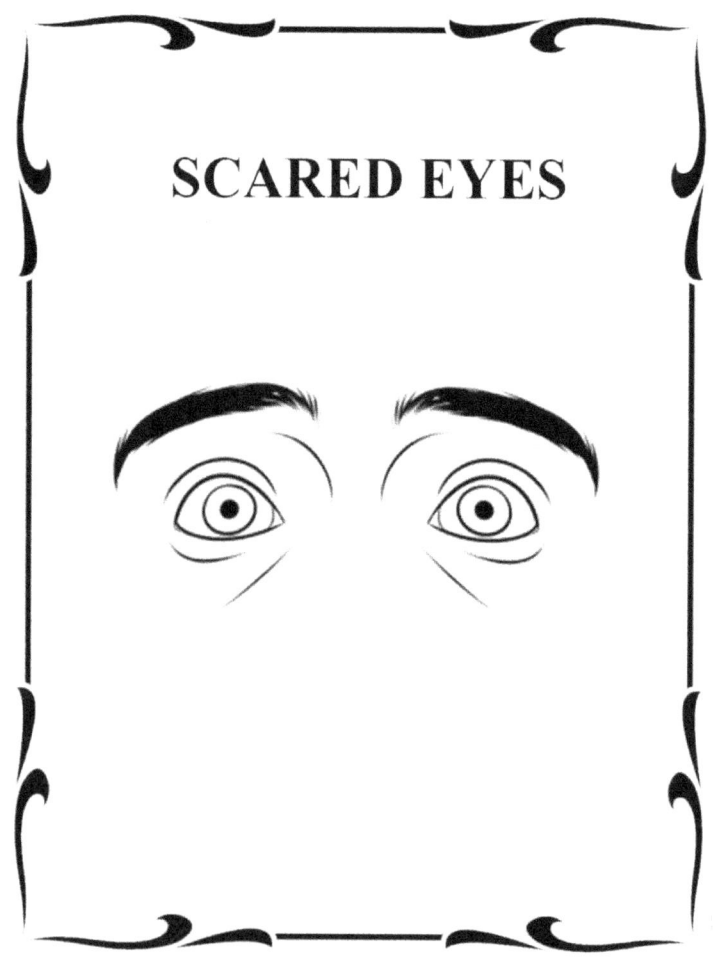

STEP 1

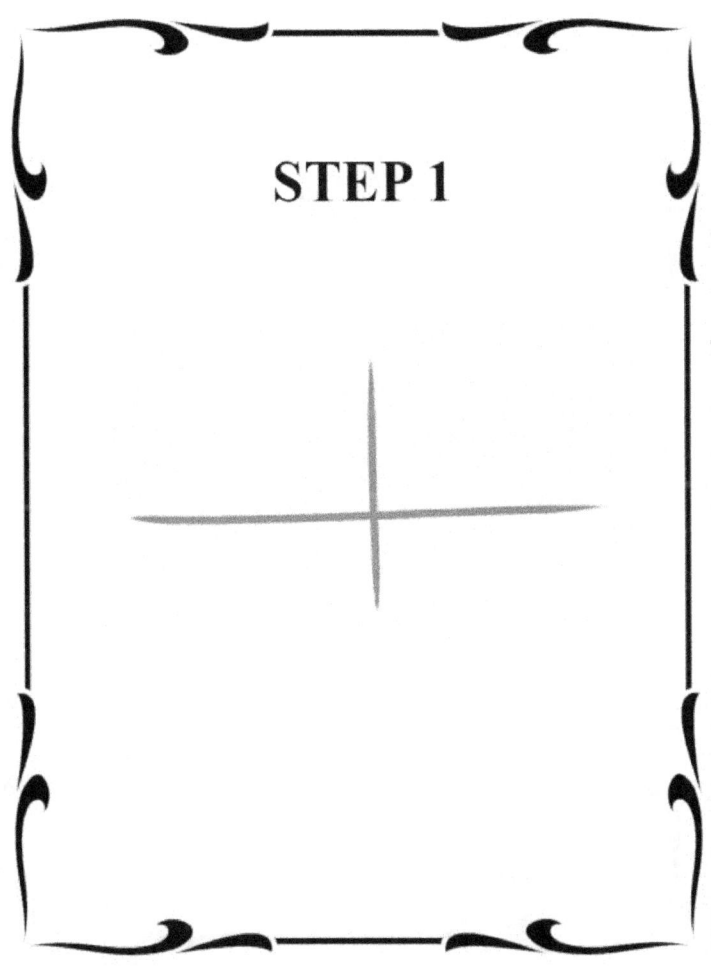

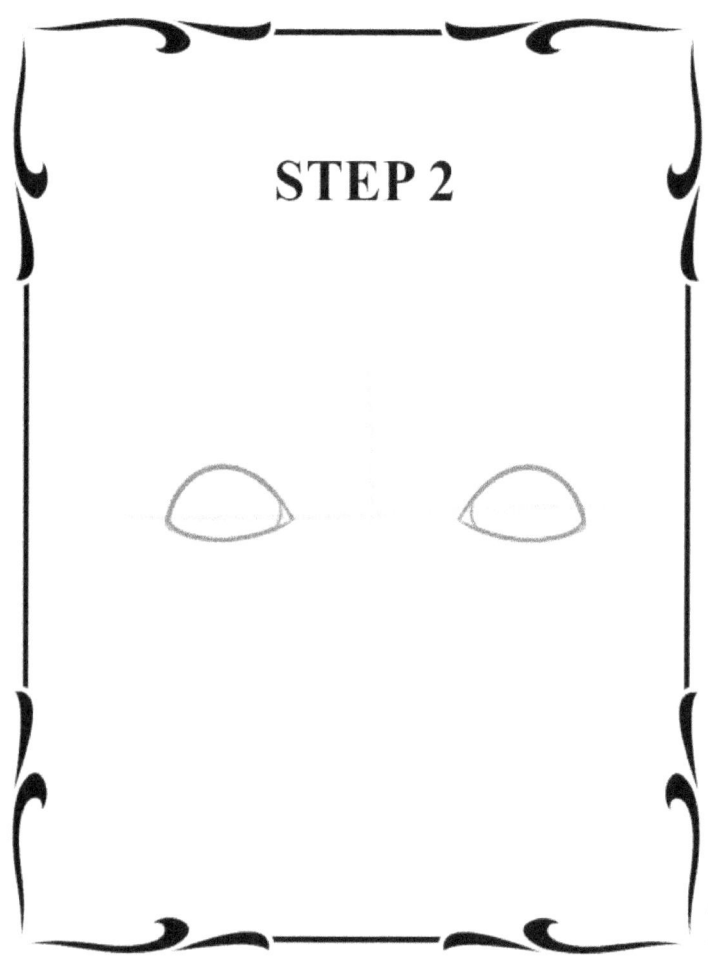

STEP 2

STEP 3

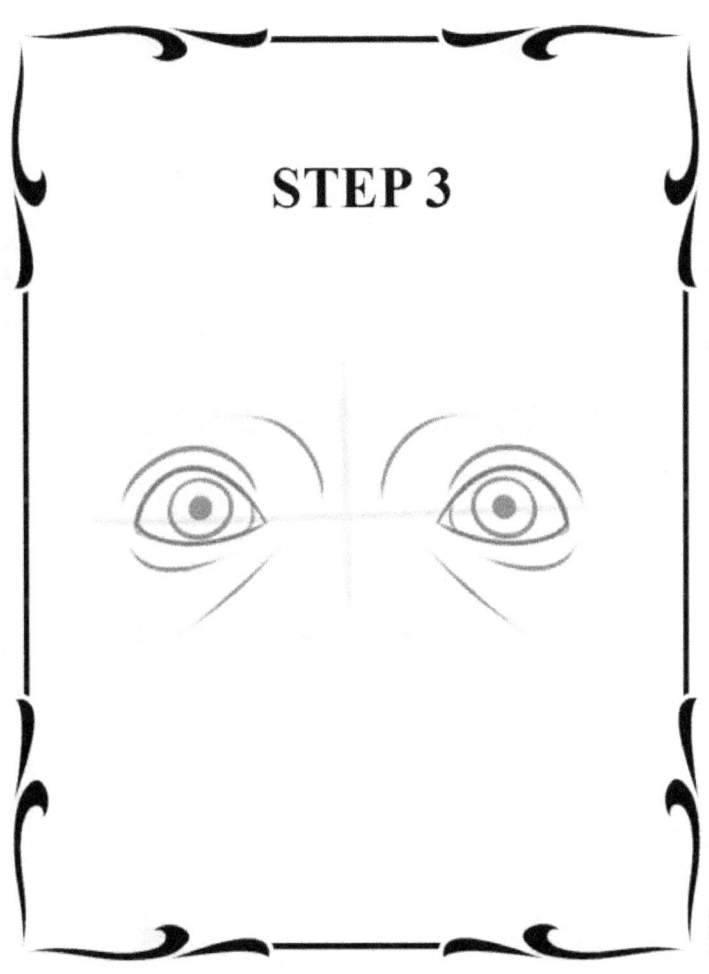

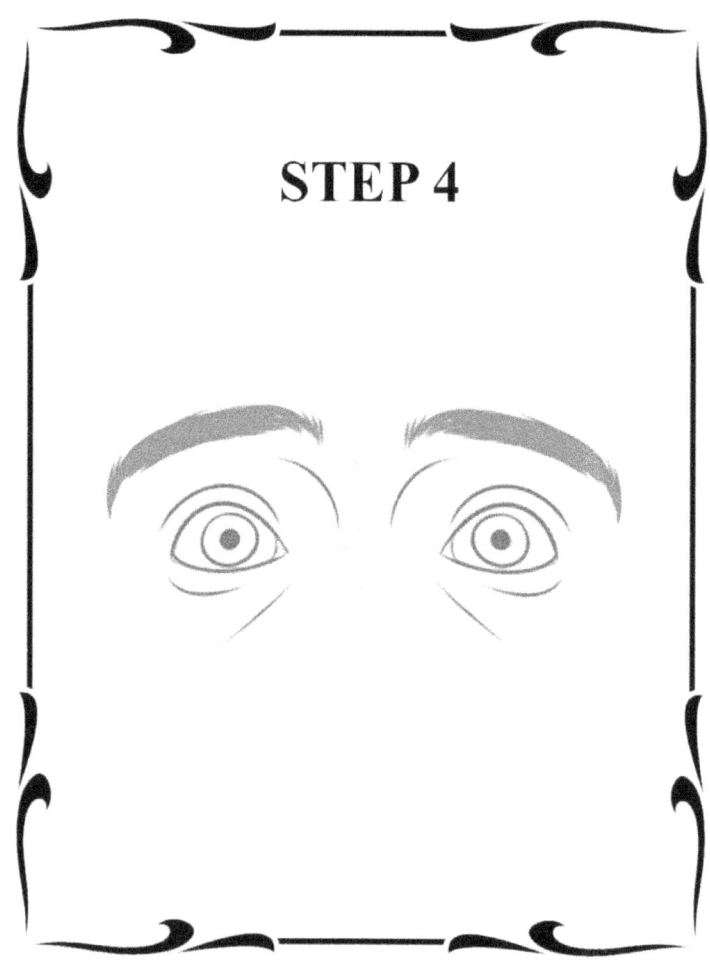

STEP 4

STEP 5

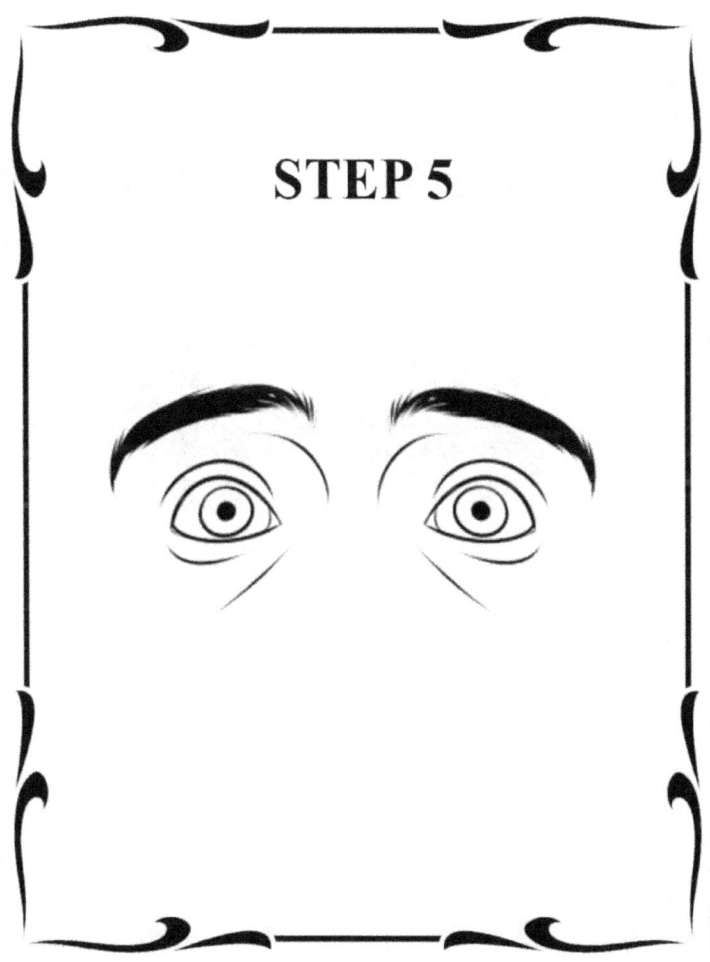

SMOKEY EYES

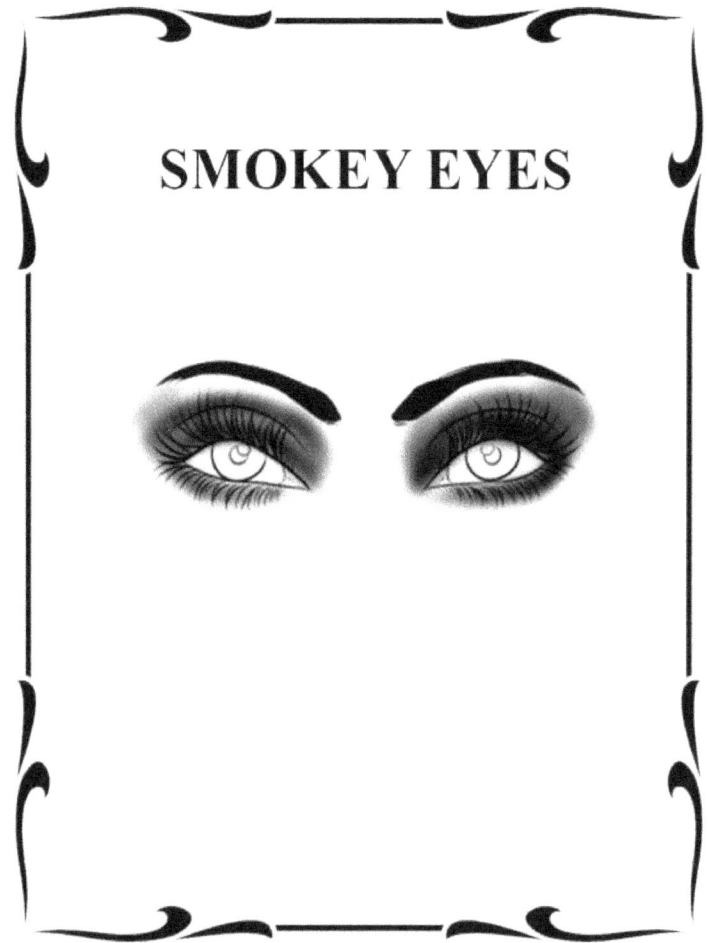

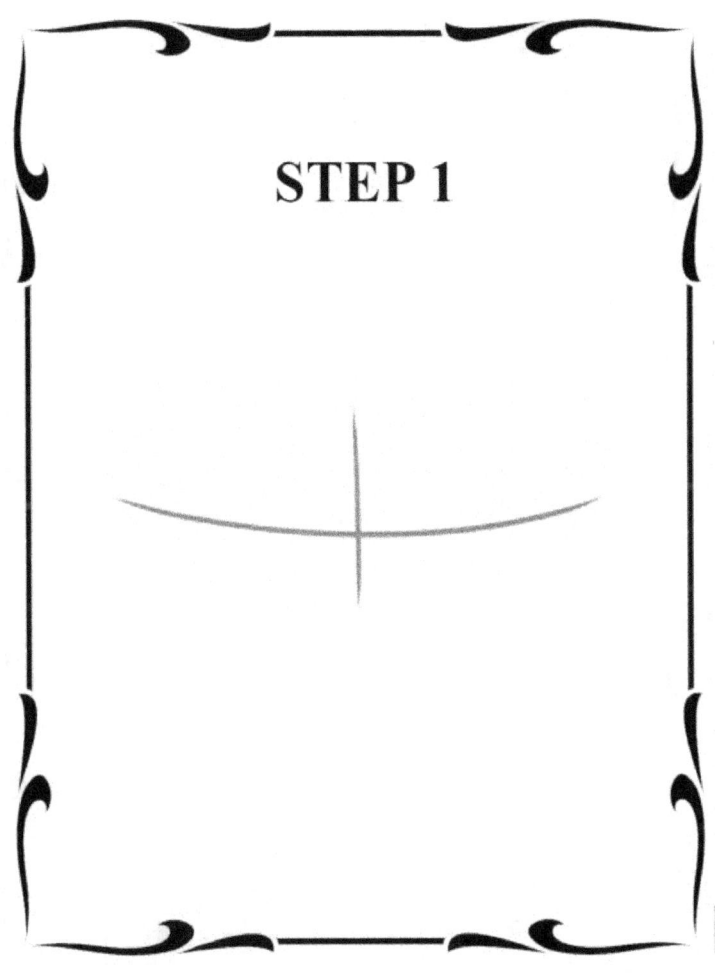

STEP 1

STEP 2

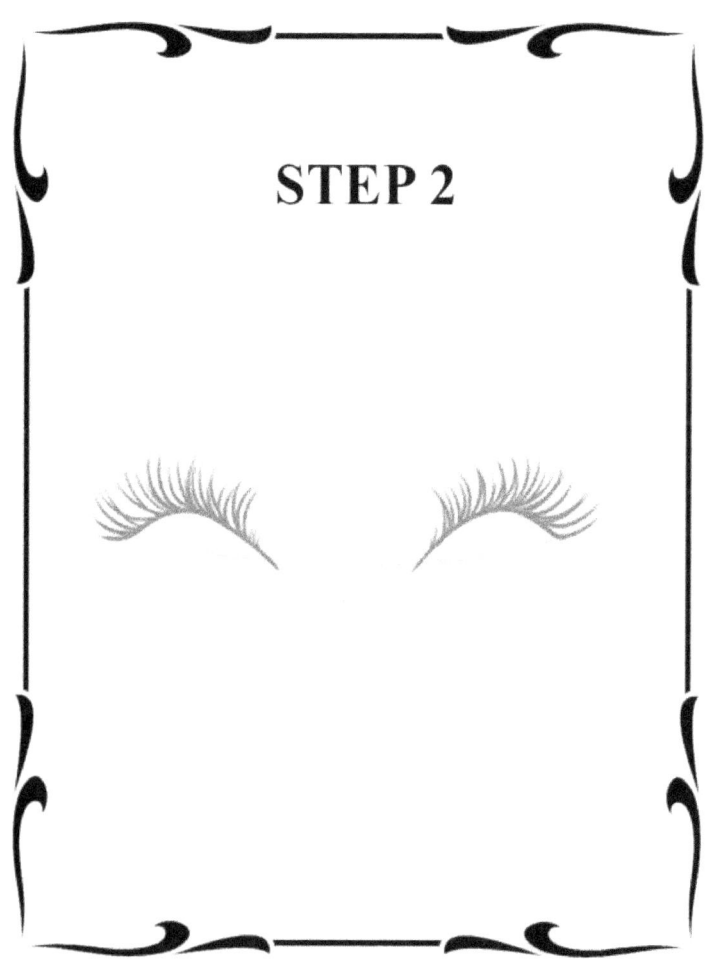

STEP 3

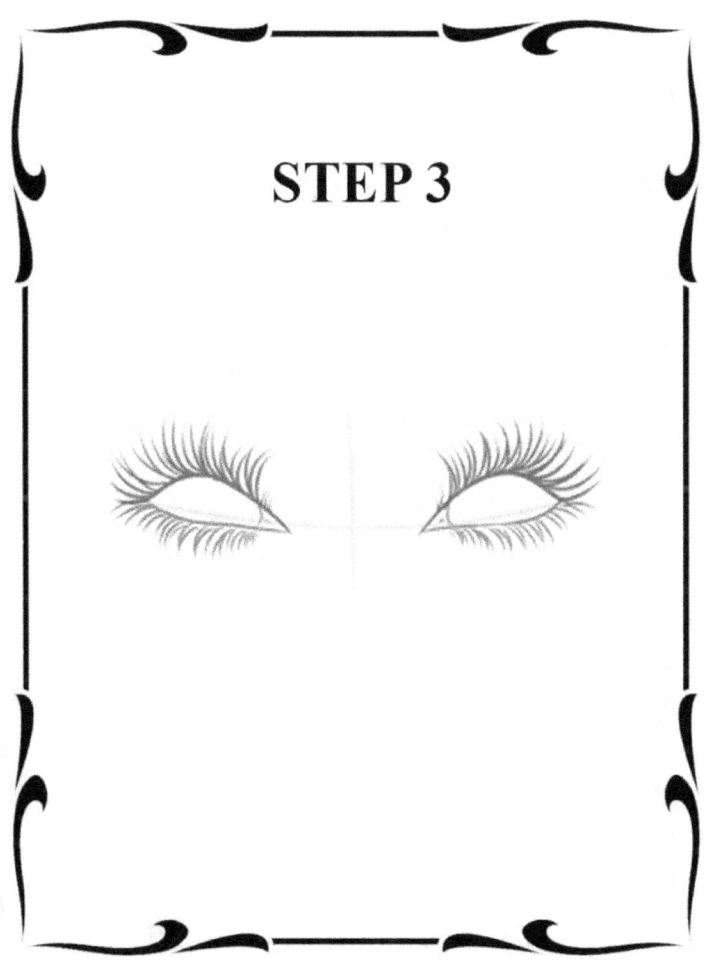

STEP 4

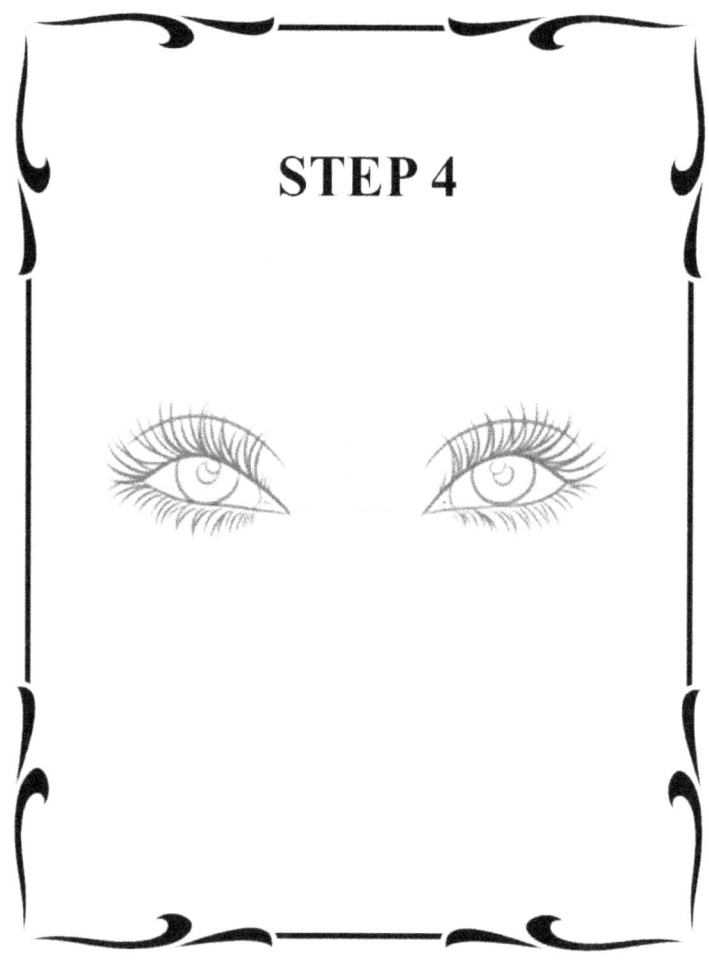

STEP 5

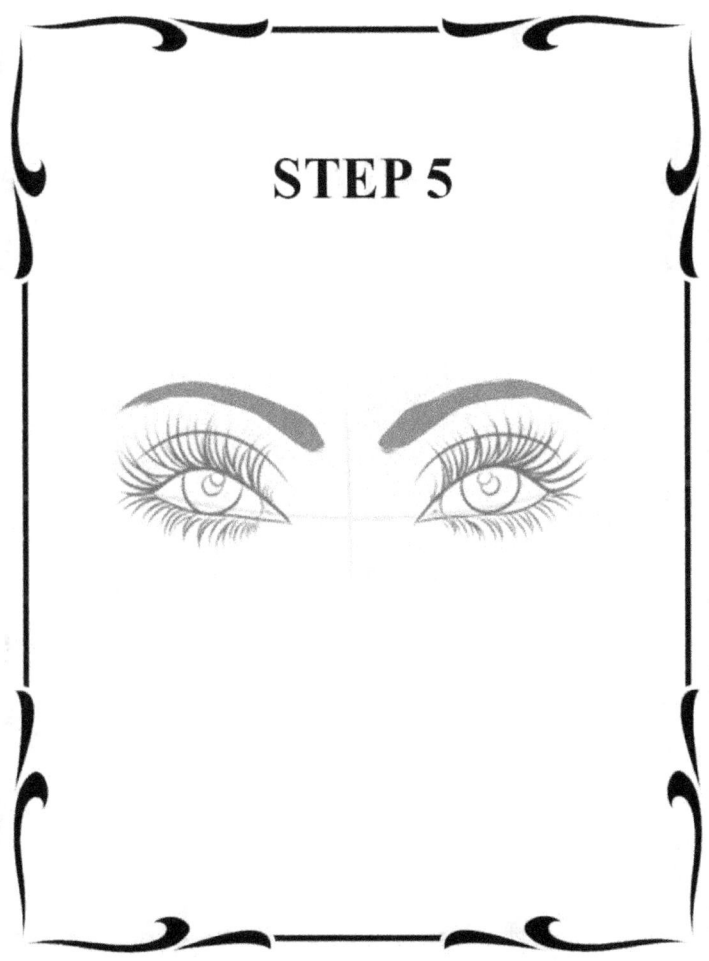

STEP 6

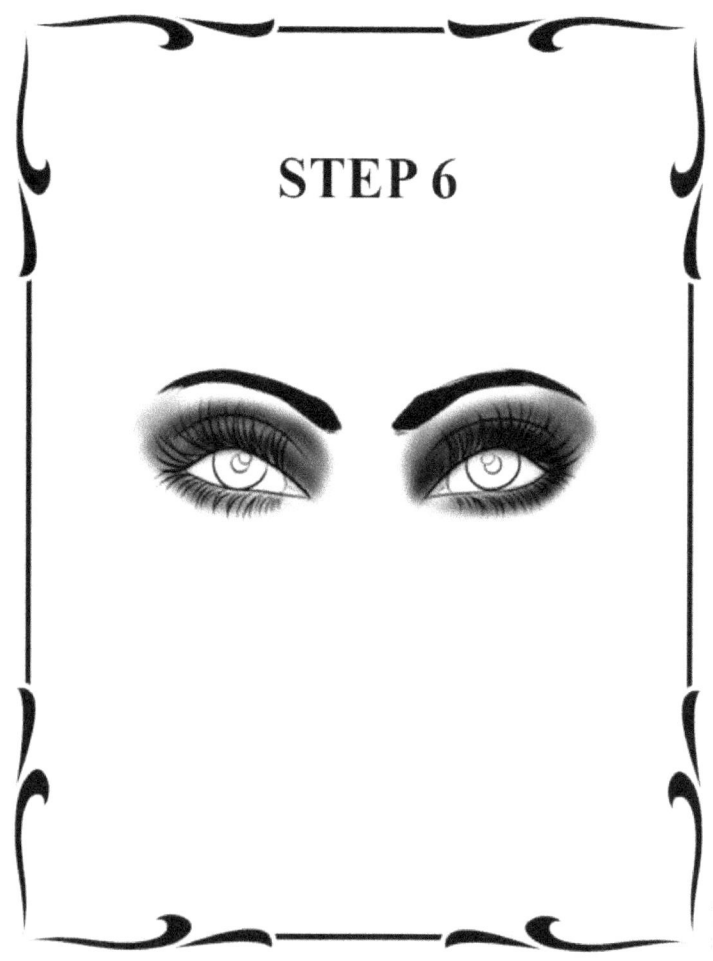

VILLAINESS EYES

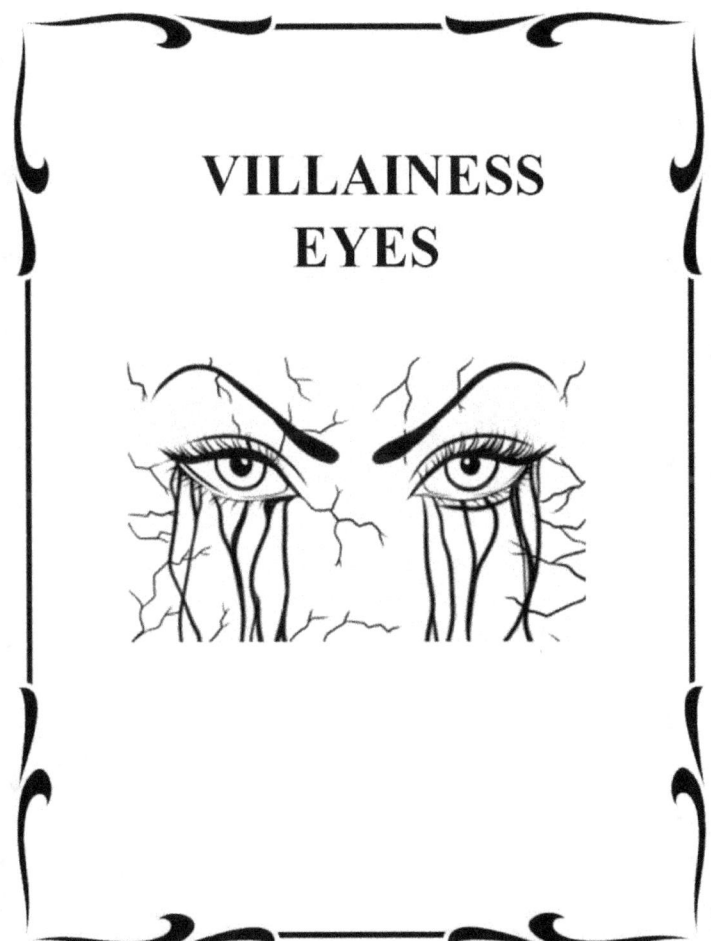

STEP 1

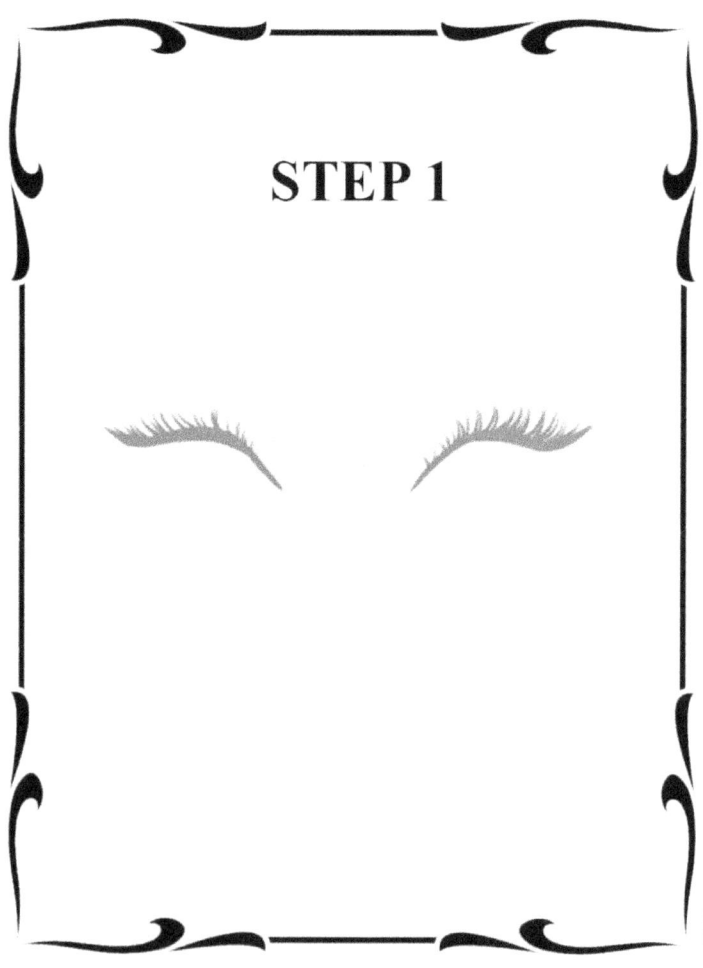

STEP 2

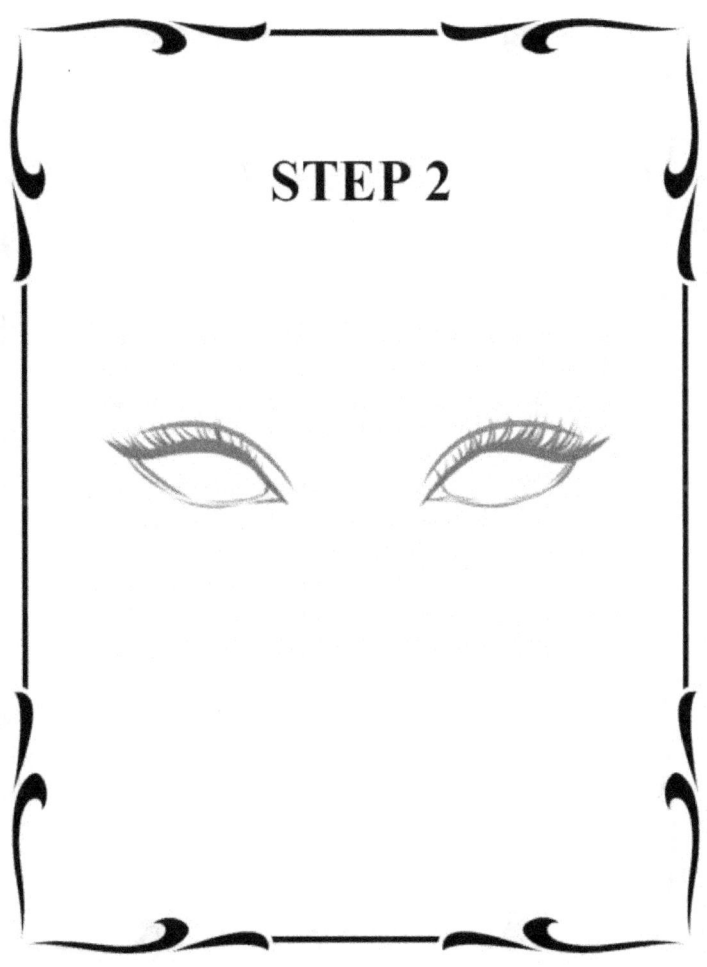

STEP 3

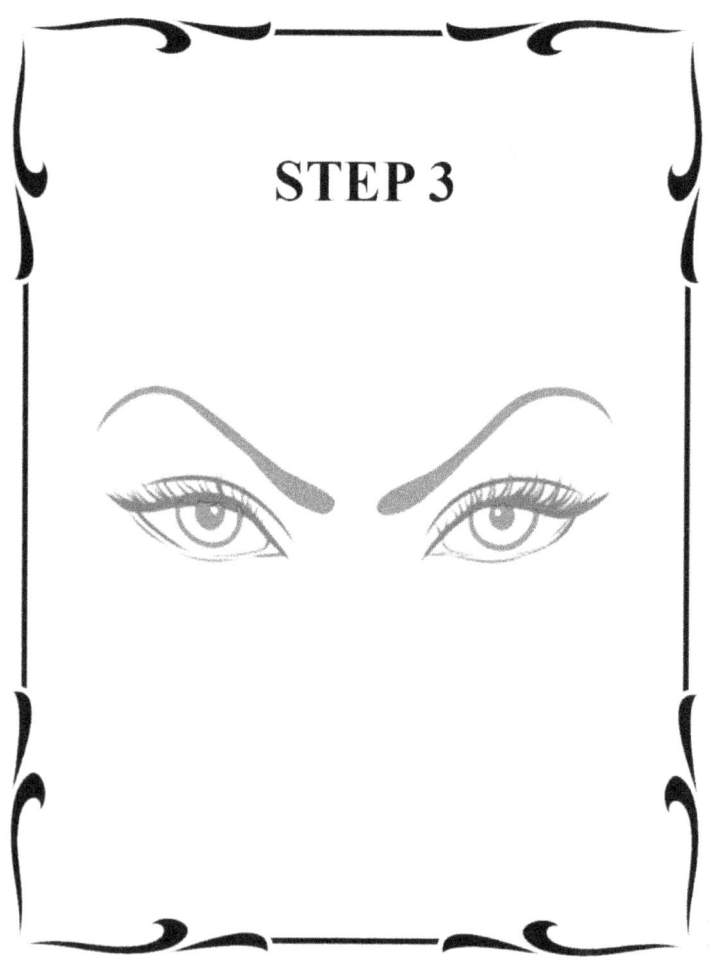

STEP 4

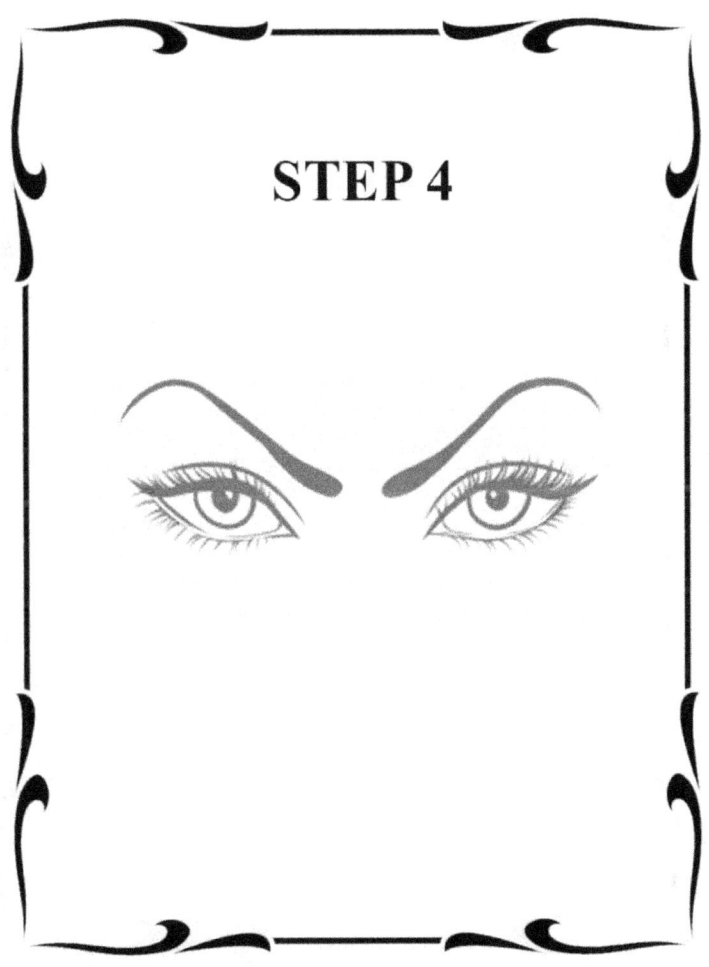

STEP 5

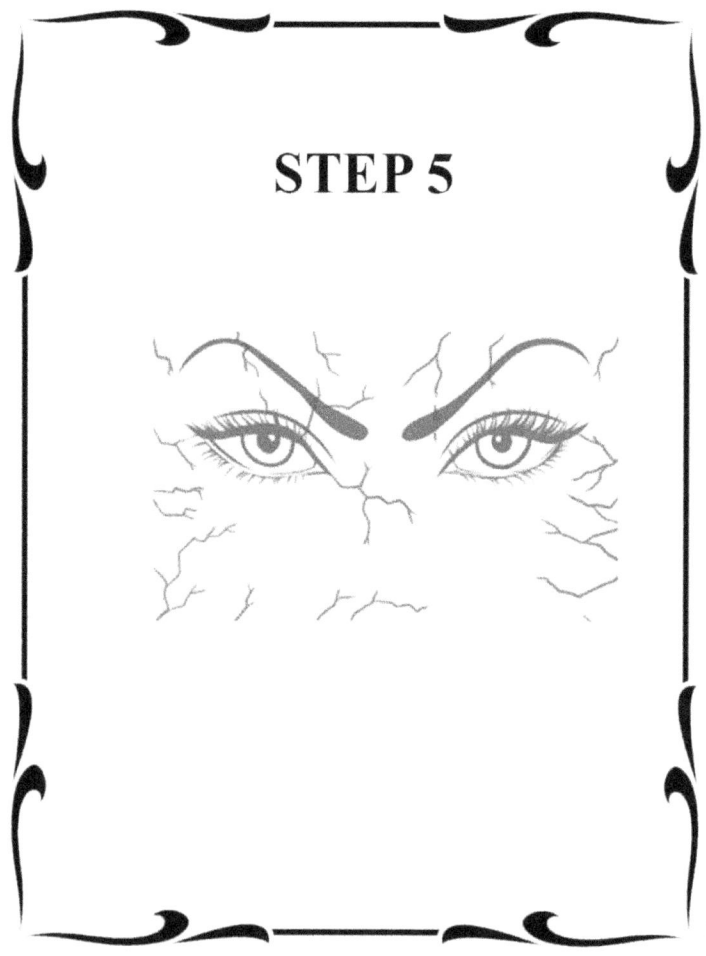

STEP 6

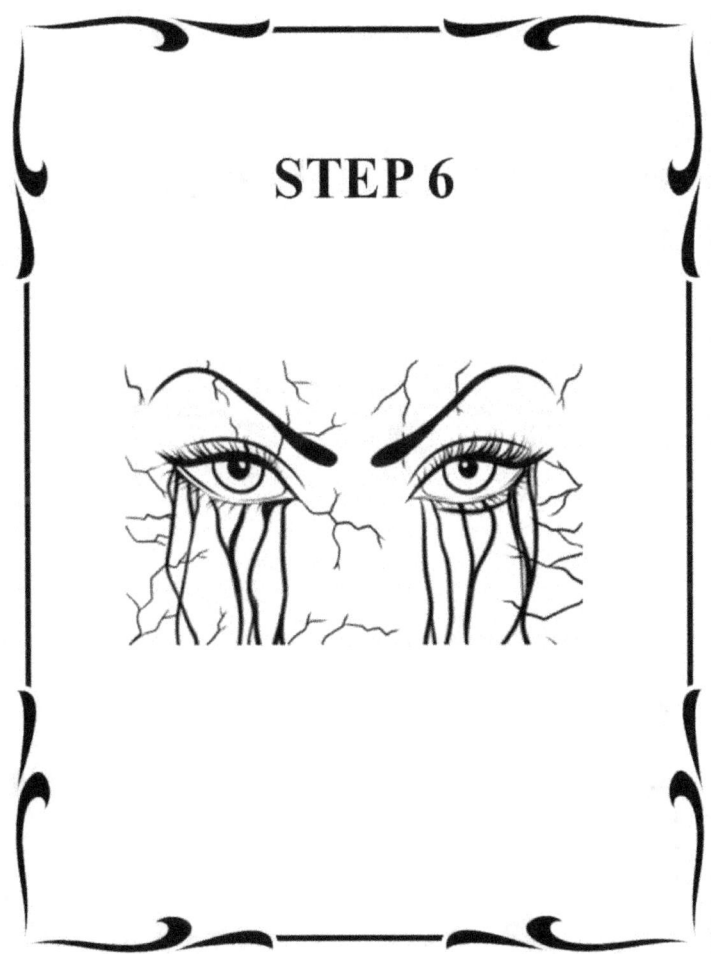

WARRIOR EYES

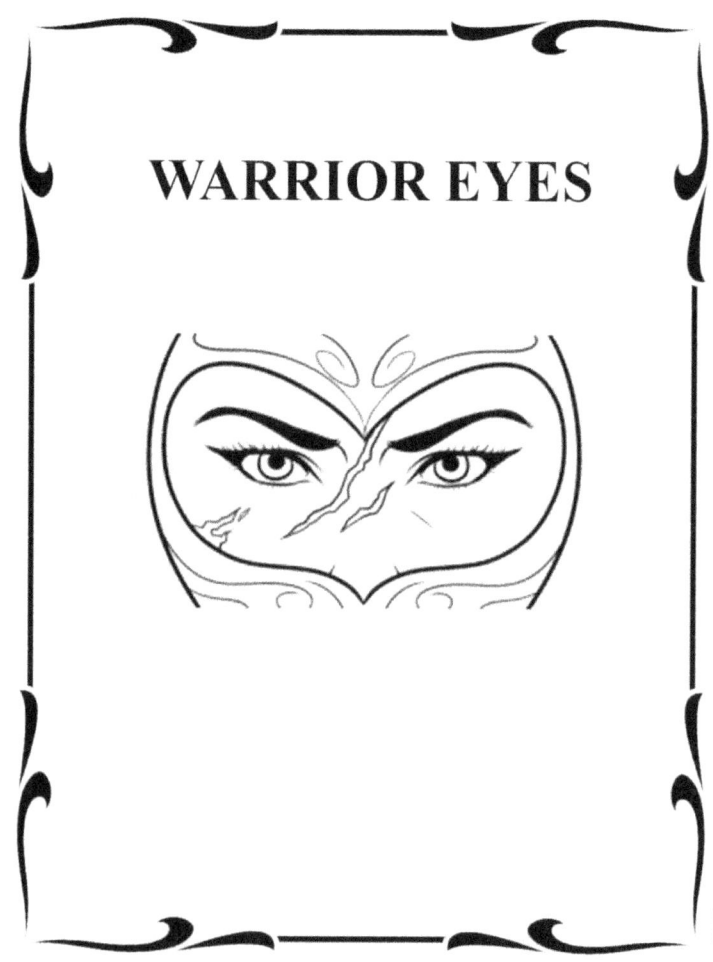

STEP 1

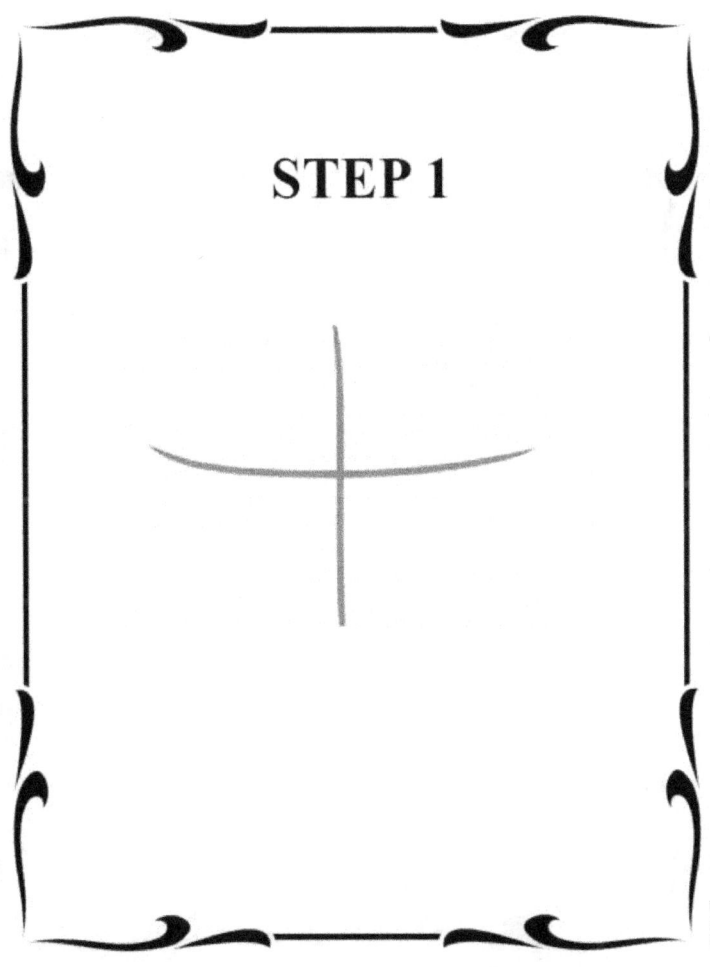

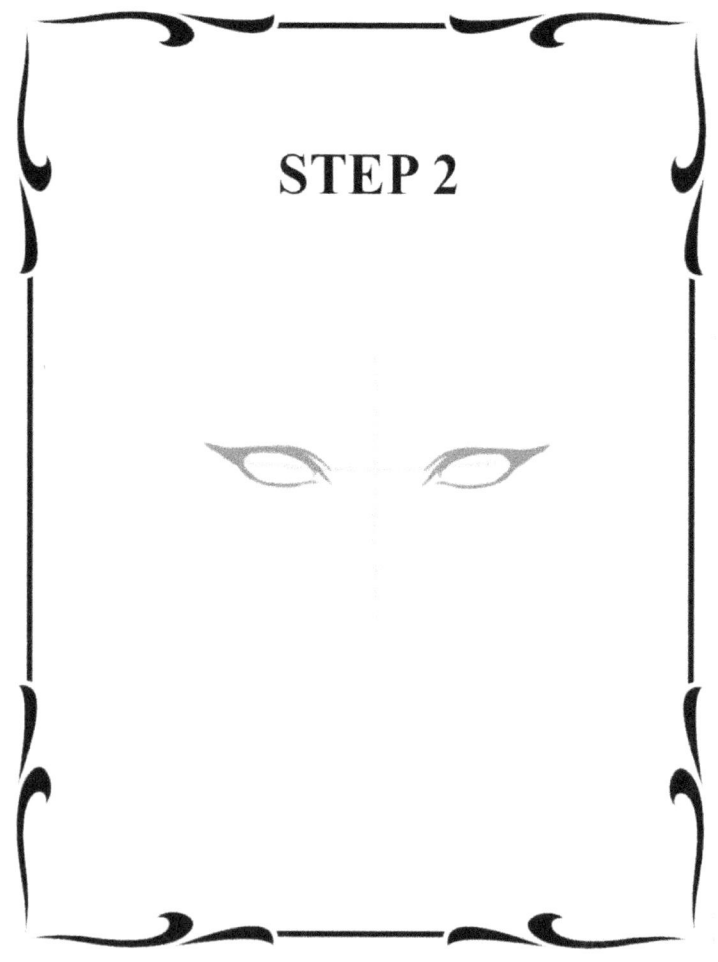

STEP 2

STEP 3

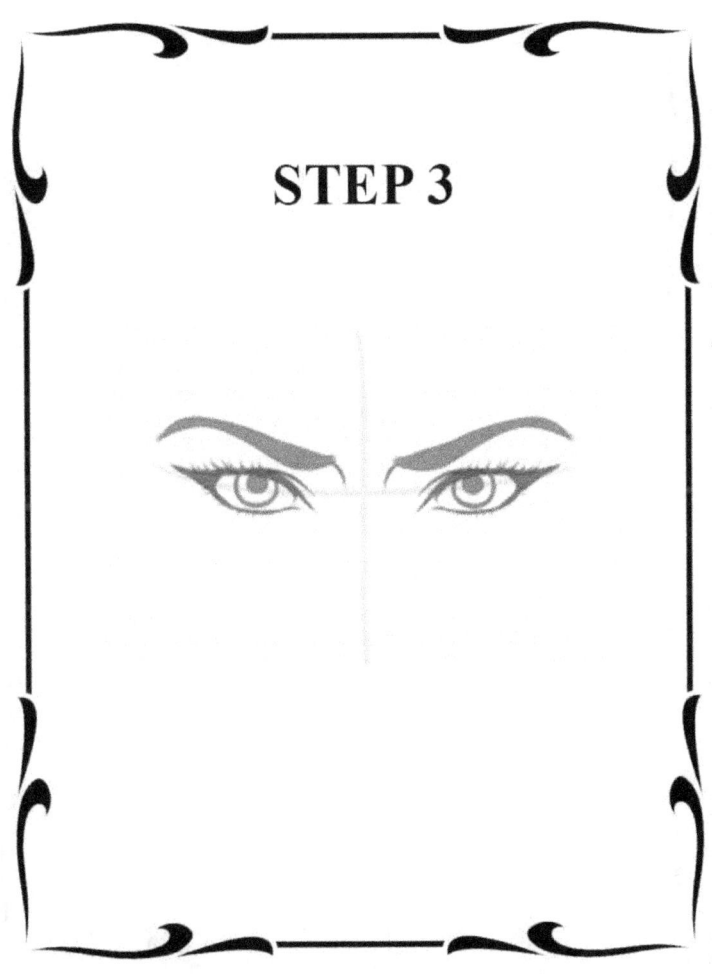

STEP 4

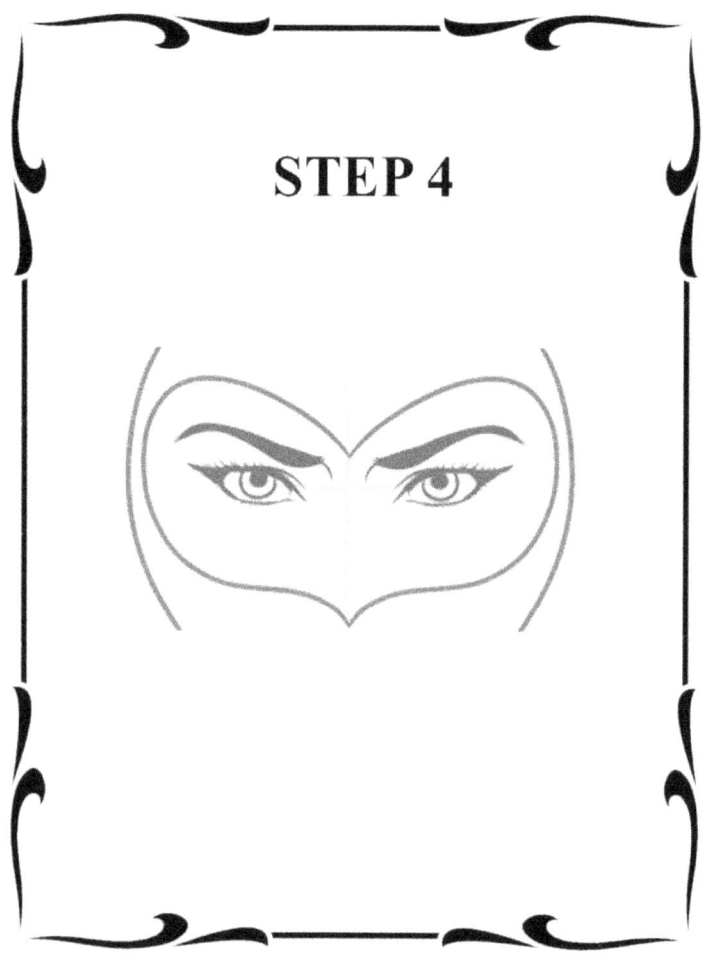

STEP 5

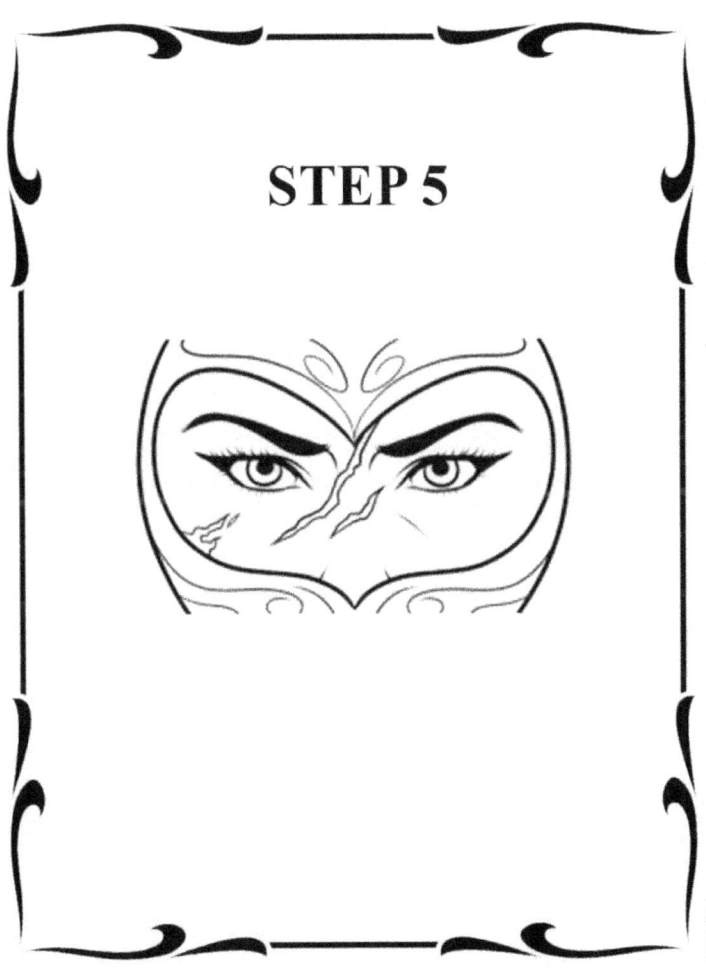

www.ingramcontent.com/pod-product-compliance
Lightning Source LLC
Chambersburg PA
CBHW071636170526
45166CB00003B/1340